Seven Steps *to* HIM Compliance

Ruthann Russo, JD, ART

Opus Communications
Marblehead, Massachusetts

Seven Steps to HIM Compliance is published by Opus Communications.

Copyright 1998 by Opus Communications, Inc.

All rights reserved. Printed in the United States of America. 5 4 3 2 1

ISBN 1-57839-043-5

Except where specifically encouraged, no part of this publication may be reproduced, in any form or by any means, without prior written consent of Opus Communications or the Copyright Clearance Center (978/750-8400). Please notify us immediately if you have received an unauthorized copy. Arrangements can be made for quantity discounts.

Opus Communications provides information resources for the health care industry. Opus Communications is not affiliated in any way with the Joint Commission on Accreditation of Healthcare Organizations.

Jennifer I. Cofer, Executive Publisher
Rob Stuart, Publisher
Ruthann Russo, JD, ART, Author
Kristen Woods, Executive Editor
Claudia Hoffacker, Editor
Meaghan Dwyer, Associate Editor
Jean St. Pierre, Art Director
Mike Mirabello, Graphic Artist
Tom Philbrook, Cover Designer

Advice given is general. Readers should check federal and state requirements to ensure that their health information management programs follow those guidelines. Consult professional counsel for specific legal, ethical, or clinical questions.

For more information on this or other Opus Communications' publications, contact:

Opus Communications
P.O. Box 1168
Marblehead, MA 01945
Telephone: 800/650-6787 or 781/639-1872
Fax: 800/639-8511 or 781/639-2982
E-mail: customer_service@opuscomm.com

Visit the Opus Communications World Wide Web site: www.opuscomm.com

TABLE OF CONTENTS

About the Author v

Introduction: Getting Started 3

Step 1: Understanding the Big Picture 9

Step 2: Forming Your Compliance Team 19
    Exhibit 2.1: HIM Compliance Manager Responsibilities 22
    Exhibit 2.2: HIM Compliance Team Agenda 28
    Exhibit 2.3: HIM Compliance Communication Flowchart 31
    Exhibit 2.4: HIM Compliance Program Employee
                    Communication Survey 33

Step 3: Developing Your Standards of Conduct 39
    Exhibit 3.1: Contents of the Standards of Conduct 40
    Exhibit 3.2: Preamble to AHIMA's Code of Ethics and Bylaws . . . 43
    Exhibit 3.3: AHIMA's Standards of Ethical Coding 45
    Exhibit 3.4: AHIMA's CCS Coding Competencies 47
    Exhibit 3.5: AHIMA's CCS-P Coding Competencies
                    (July 1998) 50
    Exhibit 3.6: Reporting Responsibilities for All Employees 58
    Exhibit 3.7: Reporting Requirements for All Employees 59
    Exhibit 3.8: Real-life Scenarios for the Standards of Conduct. . . . 61
    Exhibit 3.9: Employee Statement of Understanding for
                    the Standards of Conduct 64

Step 4: Conducting a Compliance Assessment 69
    Exhibit 4.1: Inpatient Coding and Abstracting Process
                    Flowchart 76

Step 5: Providing Education and Training—The Hub of Compliance . . . 85
    Exhibit 5.1: The OIG's List of Compliance Issues 86
    Exhibit 5.2: Common Documentation Problems for
                    Physicians 88

Exhibit 5.3: Evaluation and Management Billing Guide 90
Exhibit 5.4: Compliance Education Session Track Sheet 96
Exhibit 5.5: Employee Attendance Track Sheet 99
Exhibit 5.6: Resources for HIM Coding Staff 100

Step 6: Ongoing Monitoring—Keeping Your House in Order . . . 105
Exhibit 6.1: Analysis of Your Current Monitoring Process . . . 106
Exhibit 6.2: Four General Guidelines for HIM Supervisors . . . 107
Exhibit 6.3: Documentation Content and Quality
Deficiency Form 112
Exhibit 6.4: Compliance Documentation Completeness
Review Form 115
Exhibit 6.5: DRG/Data Quality Audit Worksheet 120
Exhibit 6.6: HIM Compliance Release of Information
Review Form 124
Exhibit 6.7: Compliance Record Retention Audit/Review
Form 126

Step 7: Conducting a Compliance Audit 133
Exhibit 7.1: Checklist of Criteria for Auditing Firms 136
Exhibit 7.2: Data Elements to Record and Preserve 141

Epilogue 145

— About the Author —

Ruthann Russo, JD, ART, is President of the Compliance and Education Division at QuadraMed Corporation. She is responsible for creating and developing consulting services and software products that address compliance, coding, and education issues for healthcare providers. Ms. Russo has developed health information management (HIM) and billing compliance programs and audits for acute-care facilities and physician groups across the country.

Ms. Russo is certified as an Accredited Record Technician (ART) by the American Health Information Management Association (AHIMA) and is a member of the New Jersey and Pennsylvania Bars. She holds a bachelor of arts degree in Liberal Arts from Dickinson College, Carlisle, PA and a Juris Doctorate (JD) from American University, Washington, DC. Currently, Ms. Russo is pursuing a graduate degree in Public Health at the University of Medicine and Dentistry of New Jersey.

— INTRODUCTION —

Getting Started

— INTRODUCTION —

Getting Started

The health information management (HIM) professional plays a key role in developing an effective healthcare corporate compliance program (CCP). If the federal government targets your organization for a fraud and abuse investigation, the HIM department is the first stop on its list. It's up to you, the HIM director, to make sure your department is in compliance with state and federal laws, regulations, and guidelines.

Why do you need this book?

Seven Steps to HIM Compliance will help you to develop an effective HIM compliance program that fits your organization's unique culture and complements its system-wide CCP. It draws on resources such as the Health and Human Services' Office of the Inspector General's (OIG) *Compliance Program Guidance for Hospitals.* With this book, you will be able to develop a program that meets federal laws and regulations, as well as most state guidelines. It is wise, however, to check your state's specific requirements to ensure that your program follows those guidelines.

Seven Steps to HIM Compliance will help you to
- understand the basics of compliance and the components of a CCP;
- form your HIM compliance team;
- develop HIM standards of conduct;
- identify potential risk areas in your realm of responsibility, and conduct compliance assessments;
- create an effective compliance education program;
- implement an ongoing monitoring process for all of your risk areas; and

- select the audit methodologies that are most suited to your organization and department.

How is this book organized?

This book is organized into seven steps that will help you to create and develop your HIM compliance program. Each step is critical to the compliance process; you do not have to accomplish or develop them in any particular order. However, you should read through this entire handbook carefully before beginning.

Step 1 contains a general overview of compliance to help you understand the "big picture" and get you started on developing your program. **Step 2** offers guidance on forming your compliance team. **Step 3** will help you to develop a standards of conduct statement, one of the most important components of your compliance program.

Step 4 shows you how to assess your department's workflow and identify potential risk areas. This assessment will allow you to determine where you should focus your efforts during the initial phases of compliance implementation. You should address activities with a higher risk potential first. Along with Step 2, Step 4 plays a key role in shaping the framework of your program.

You will learn how to educate your HIM staff, as well as members of other departments that are involved in compliance in **Step 5.** In **Step 6** you will learn how to conduct an ongoing monitoring review in your HIM department. This ongoing review, along with the regular external auditing process detailed in **Step 7,** will help you ensure that your department maintains compliance.

Start with the right frame of mind

As you begin to develop your new HIM compliance program or refine your existing one, remember that the OIG states in its *Compliance Program Guidance for Hospitals* that "compliance makes good business sense." This should be enough to justify your investment in an effective compliance program. We hope that as you begin your creative process, you will embrace compliance as a go-forward strategy that "makes good business sense" in managing your HIM department.

— STEP 1 —

Understanding the Big Picture

Before you start to build your program, you must clearly understand what the term "compliance" means. In the most basic sense, compliance entails running a business according to the laws, regulations, and guidelines that govern it.

Healthcare compliance

Although compliance is a relatively new concept to the healthcare industry, almost every other industry in America has embraced it over the last 30 years. Usually, compliance is kicked off by a government initiative and then becomes part of the core of an industry. This was true in the communications, environmental, and defense industries.

In the healthcare industry, compliance can be a bit more complex because of the large number of laws and administrative regulations that govern the delivery of, and payment for, services. Couple the private payer and managed care contractual obligations with accreditation standards, and compliance can seem like an impossibility to any healthcare provider. That's why it's so important for every healthcare organization to have a formal program dedicated to keeping the organization in compliance.

Medical record documentation is the heart of healthcare. It serves as the basis for present and future patient treatment, as well as a basis for the research and development of new treatments. Documentation helps assess the quality of care provided to the patient. It also determines billing and reimbursement for the provider's services.

All of these reasons show how important documentation is to the compliance process. But in today's environment of constant audits for Medicare fraud by the Office of the Inspector General (OIG), the third reason—reimbursement—shows that documentation could be the key to steering clear of multimillion-dollar fines and penalties. Whether patient care is reimbursed by Medicare, Medicaid, private payers, or a health maintenance organization (HMO), the documentation of that care is at the core of the reimbursement process. And it's up to the health information management (HIM) professional to ensure that medical record documentation is thorough, accurate, and completed in a timely manner.

As a result of the federal government's infamous Physicians at Teaching Hospitals (PATH) settlement with the Clinical Practices of the University of Pennsylvania in 1995, the OIG now consistently states, "If it's not documented, it wasn't performed." This statement has become the mantra of HIM professionals—it simply highlights how critical documentation is to compliance.

The importance of the medical record

Several federal settlements with healthcare organizations illustrate the importance of medical records in appropriate reimbursement. In 1987, the federal government and the State of Colorado, through the Medicaid program, entered into an $800,000 settlement with the University Physicians of the University of Colorado. This settled an outstanding claim by Medicaid that the University Physicians had billed for services not rendered. The state based its claim on the fact that billings weren't substantiated by medical record documentation. From 1987 to 1995, similar claims from government agencies were generally nonexistent.

Then in December 1995, the Clinical Practices of the University of Pennsylvania entered into a $30 million settlement with the OIG for alleged overbilling. The OIG claimed that the physicians billed for residents' services provided without the required physician supervision. It also said the physicians submitted bills for which there was insufficient documentation or no documentation to substantiate services provided. Under the False Claims Act, the federal government can assess civil penalties up to $10,000 per claim, plus triple damages. In the case of CPUP, the settlement involved a tripling of $10 million of alleged overbillings over the course of five years.

The 1995 University of Pennsylvania settlement set off a host of similar settlements with Thomas Jefferson University, the University of Pittsburgh, and SmithKline Beecham Clinical Laboratories, with many more settlements pending. The Federal Sentencing Guidelines, developed by the U.S. Sentencing Commission to be used as standards for sentencing criminal defendants in federal criminal cases, were the basis for each of these settlements. These 12 guidelines follow a point system that reduces or increases an organization's criminal exposure risk depending on whether it has complied with each of the guidelines. From the healthcare provider's perspective, complying with every guideline can decrease an organization's fines and exposure by up to 95%.

In the last two years, the OIG has provided additional guidance to the healthcare industry by publishing three model compliance plans—one for laboratories, one for hospitals, and one for home health agencies. Models for other healthcare settings are in the works. In its model plans, the OIG focuses on coding, billing, documentation, and the completeness of the patient's medical record. This is further evidence of the HIM department's significant role in compliance. In addition to focusing on coding and billing, the most recent OIG plan—the *Compliance Program Guidance for Hospitals*—stresses that coders must have access to complete medical records at the time of initial coding. If healthcare providers follow these guidelines, they will not only improve the quality of their billing and coding, but they could also contribute to an increase in the quality of patient care. That's why healthcare organizations need to actively get their own compliance programs in order.

Developing a compliance program

By now, most providers should at least have some prototype of a compliance program in place for each of its facilities. An organization should assess the effectiveness of its program regularly. Within the next five years, the healthcare industry should enter into a period of relative maturity in which comprehensive compliance programs are part of the framework of every provider.

Become your compliance officer's best friend

You need to work closely with your organization's compliance officer as you develop a compliance program for the HIM department. The compliance officer–HIM director relationship is one of the most beneficial, symbiotic relationships that can exist for an organization. Chances are your compliance officer is not an HIM professional. In a recent QuadraMed survey of 1,000 hospitals, 78% of all current compliance officers had legal backgrounds, 20% had financial backgrounds, and the remainder had billing, medical, or administrative backgrounds.

As a result, the HIM director is an invaluable resource to the compliance officer. He or she can provide direction and an expert response on coding and other related areas of exposure. In return, the compliance officer is often the means for the HIM department to add staff to ensure HIM compliance functions are rolled out in the most effective manner throughout the organization.

Standards of conduct

The core of any compliance program is the development of

"standards of conduct." Standards of conduct should reflect the unique culture of an organization. And each department in the organization involved in compliance should develop its own standards of conduct consistent with the corporation's overall standards.

It is common for individual departments to develop and tailor their own versions of their organization's mission, vision, and core ideology. This makes the statements even more real to the staff members in each department. Although a bit more complex, developing standards of conduct for a department is very similar to this process.

Bringing the standards of conduct to the department level is even more important from a compliance perspective. Compliance is everyone's job; each staff member must ensure compliance within his or her span of control. As a manager, you should embrace any methodology that can make the concept of compliance "real" to your staff members.

A standards of conduct statement is the document that provides ethical direction to employees. As such, the standards must have meaning to each employee who reads them and is expected to abide by them. **Step 3** addresses the development of standards of conduct for the HIM department in more detail.

The four pillars of compliance

The standards of conduct statement is the nucleus of your compliance program. It is supported by the "four pillars of compliance," the activities that make up the bulk of the compliance process. They are
- education;
- monitoring;
- auditing; and
- the written plan/policies and procedures.

Because each pillar plays a significant role in the compliance process, you can develop any of them first. Study the culture of your institution and your department. Start with whichever pillar you feel your staff will most readily understand or accept.

For example, many providers find education the best pillar with which to begin the compliance process. It is relatively benign and easy to standardize. Also, the OIG's *Compliance Program Guidance* recommends that providers educate every employee about compliance at least annually. Those employees who might place the facility at higher compliance risk (e.g., coding and billing staff) should receive compliance education "regularly." **Step 5** addresses our specific recommendations for education.

Other organizations find that it's best to start with an ongoing monitoring process **(Step 6)** and regular auditing **(Step 7).** Each step discusses the processes within the HIM department that you need to monitor and audit, outlining appropriate sample selection techniques, review and data collection tolls, and reporting and retention practices.

The written plan: proceed with caution

Many providers believe that before they can get started with a compliance program, they have to write a comprehensive compliance plan. This is simply not true. In fact, writing a compliance plan before implementing your standards of conduct or the four pillars of compliance can place your facility at higher risk. But once you do begin writing your compliance plan, you must remember two cardinal rules:

1. Write only in the present tense.
2. Do what you say you're going to do.

The first rule—write only in the present tense—addresses the risk inherent in plans that detail a comprehensive set of compliance techniques before the techniques are actually in place. Your plan is better if it's silent on any futuristic plans you might have. It is permissible, and more appropriate, to amend the plan as often as necessary. You will probably amend your plan quite frequently in the beginning stages of your planning process. Therefore, you might want to write your plan after you have developed the monitoring, auditing, and education processes. This echoes the essence of the second rule—do what you say you're going to do.

The big picture in review

Here's what you learned in **Step 1:**

- Compliance means "managing your department according to the laws, regulations, and guidelines that govern it."

- Standards of conduct are the core of your compliance program.

- The two cardinal rules of writing a compliance plan are

    1. write only in the present tense; and
    2. do what you say you're going to do.

— STEP 2 —

Forming Your Compliance Team

— Step 2 —

Forming Your Compliance Team

Developing a health information management (HIM) compliance program is a team effort; everyone in your department must embrace "compliance." As the coach, your first responsibility is to identify your front-line team. Your team should include individuals who have defined roles for ensuring that the entire department understands and embraces your HIM compliance program. As with any team effort, the members need to understand how and why compliance benefits the department and your organization. Then, they need to support compliance as a part of your department's framework.

Who should be on the team?

Compliance needs special leaders. As you decide on the make-up of your HIM compliance team, you might want to consider what the Office of the Inspector General (OIG) has said about healthcare compliance officers. Use this guidance to help you select your department's compliance team members.

According to the OIG, a potential compliance officer's specific education and credentials are not as important as his or her skills, values, and personality. While the OIG does not dictate what the background of the ideal compliance officer should be, its model plan details that a facility's compliance officer should not report to (or be) either the chief financial officer (CFO) or the general counsel. A CFO or general counsel can become a compliance officer, but no one should hold any two of these three roles simultaneously. A compliance officer is supposed to be the objective third party; an active CFO or general counsel does not have the impartiality that is necessary for the compliance function. The compliance officer is, however, expected to communicate and regularly interact with individuals in the financial and legal departments within the facility.

Let's look at the essence of the compliance role. The compliance officer is charged with ensuring that all functions within a facility comply with federal and state laws, regulations, and guidelines. He or she should pay particular attention to areas that might place the facility at noncompliance risk. This means that the compliance officer must interact with most departments within the facility. The compliance officer plays the roles of

- investigator (of potential noncompliant activities);
- negotiator (with enforcement agencies and facility departments);
- decision-maker (regarding ultimate compliance actions);
- enforcer (of adopted compliance activities);
- communicator (between parties affected by compliance); and
- analyzer (of the potential effects of any new or changed compliance activities or policies).

The compliance officer must balance all of these roles against the responsibilities of the department directors. As such, the ideal compliance officer is not an individual who seeks power and ultimate authority, but rather an individual who can enforce and coordinate compliance initiatives through cooperation.

Seeing your staff as a compliance team

You must conduct the same sort of analysis to choose the best individuals to lead the HIM department's compliance effort. HIM compliance team members perform highly sensitive and significant tasks. While many of the same activities that dominate the HIM professional's daily life will continue, they will take on an added importance as part of the compliance effort. These activities include

- speaking with physicians or other clinicians regarding complete

documentation in the patient record;
- requesting dictations and signatures for the patient record; and
- reviewing the patient record to ensure that the documentation supports the coding assignment.

While your staff members have most likely always done these and other tasks as part of the HIM function, they must now document them as part of the department's compliance plan. You should document regular monitoring, auditing, and education for each of these activities.

At some point, you must determine how many team members you'll need to handle all of the compliance activities. It might be difficult to arrive at an accurate number before you have actually begun to implement the education and monitoring activities. In the meantime, you should appoint a compliance manager to lead your team. That manager could be you (the HIM director) or another manager within your department. Remember, however, that even if you are not the compliance manager, you still need to be intimately involved in the compliance process. See Exhibit 2.1 for a list of HIM compliance manager responsibilities.

One important member of your team is an appointed secretary—usually a leader in one of the risk areas or even the compliance manager. The secretary should be someone who can clearly and concisely document meetings and decisions. Fastidious recordkeeping should happen at every meeting; preservation of this documentation is key to the compliance process.

What skills do team members need?
While your facility's compliance officer doesn't need to have training in a specific academic discipline, your HIM compliance team members do. Your compliance leaders must have expertise in the

Exhibit 2.1

HIM Compliance Manager Responsibilities

The health information management (HIM) compliance manager serves under the direction of the compliance committee and the corporate compliance manager. He or she coordinates the development, implementation, and updating of the compliance program as it relates to HIM coding and associated functions such as billing integrity.

The HIM compliance manager has the following responsibilities:

- Develops testing methods to monitor compliance with coding policies and procedures and conducts periodic audits of coding practices to ensure accurate abstracting, inpatient and outpatient coding, and record completeness.

- Reports to the compliance committee regularly regarding the status of the HIM compliance program and any monitoring activity results.

- Develops, coordinates, and participates in programs to educate and train all appropriate employees, managers, and medical staff about the HIM coding compliance program, as well as Medicare's coding requirements.

- Acquires and maintains expertise in appropriate use of ICD-9-CM, CPT, and HCPC codes in order to advise management on compliance-related issues.

- Advises and assists the facility's legal department in its interactions with government agencies on coding-compliance-related matters, and, with the legal department, coordinates the resolution of any coding-related investigations.

- Assists management in the annual process of updating the charge description master and assists in the process of reviewing claim rejections.

- Investigates matters related to HIM compliance and coordinates any resulting corrective actions with the facility's legal department and other appropriate personnel.

- Works closely with the facility's human resources department to
    - incorporate compliance criteria in job descriptions;
    - enforce disciplinary actions when necessary; and
    - maintain signature proof upon termination of employment signifying

Exhibit 2.1 *continued*

HIM Compliance Manager Responsibilities

that an employee has neither participated in any noncompliance activities nor witnessed the same.

- Ensures that the HIM department retains medical records in accordance with state regulations, stores them securely due to their confidential nature, and (when appropriate) destroys their contents in a manner that protects their confidentiality.

- Ensures that policies and procedures are implemented addressing the release of information (ROI) to patients, guardians, attorneys, and other third parties.

- Develops and disseminates policies and procedures that facilitate compliance with Medicare's coding requirements and that encourage managers and employees to report suspected incidents of noncompliance.

- Answers any questions that coding personnel might have that cannot be answered by HIM policies and procedures.

- Makes available and regularly updates all coding resources used by employees, such as the AHA's *Coding Handbook* and *Coding Clinic*, the AMA's *CPT Assistant*, and ICD-9-CM books.

- Informs independent contractors and agents who furnish coding-related services of the HIM compliance program's requirements, ensures that agreements with independent contractors for coding services are not on a contingency basis, and conducts background checks on the Medicare and Medicaid status of independent contractors to ensure that they are eligible for participation in those programs.

- Assists the internal audit department in HIM compliance audits.

- Coordinates external audits of coding-related functions, reports findings to the compliance committee, and implements corrective action as appropriate.

- Identifies those areas within the coding process that pose high risk in terms of potential government fines and other sanctions, and works proactively with appropriate management and staff to mitigate such risks.

areas that they will address with individuals in other departments. Without this expertise, your department risks a significant loss of credibility. And, without credibility, it is impossible to garner enough support and cooperation from the management of your facility to ensure an effective compliance program.

One important and necessary virtue is enthusiasm for the compliance process. Every member of your team needs to have a positive and enthusiastic attitude about compliance in general and HIM compliance processes specifically. The ideal individuals to lead the HIM compliance process are those with
- expertise in their area(s) of focus;
- high ethical values for work performance;
- a clear understanding of "right" versus "wrong" in business dealings; and
- the personality to elicit cooperation and understanding from parties whose goals seem to be at odds with those of the HIM department (e.g., busy physicians who need to devote more time to completely documenting patient records).

Your HIM compliance team must include individuals who command respect due to their interactive and communications skills, as well as their professional expertise. HIM staff members who have been the most successful at negotiating with physicians and other clinicians are probably your best choices.

Addressing HIM high-risk areas
In addition to selecting individuals with the right values and personality, you need to ensure that you have team members who possess the appropriate knowledge and skills in HIM compliance risk areas. The top five risk areas are
- content and quality of documentation;
- completeness of documentation;

- coding and abstracting;
- release of information (ROI); and
- record retention and storage.

While you might not need one staff member for each of these risk areas, you do want to make sure that someone on your team has expertise in one or all of these areas. For example, your current HIM team might include a staff member with expertise in coding and abstracting, as well as in the content and quality of documentation. Another member might be proficient in completeness of documentation, ROI, and record retention. Whatever the mix, it is necessary to ensure that you have representation from every area of risk on your compliance team.

In addition to the five common areas of HIM compliance risk described above, you might also have other areas of compliance risk specific to your department. **Step 4: Conducting a Compliance Assessment** addresses how to identify your own high-risk areas. But at a minimum, these five HIM activities are the areas with intrinsic compliance risk.

For example, the coding and abstracting process is inherently connected to the billing function. The OIG is focusing on the billing function (and hence coding) to assess fines under the False Claims Act.

The coding function is one that has always been at the core of the HIM profession. Before 1982, when the Prospective Payment System (PPS) was implemented, the coding process was the source for statistics and research. After PPS was in place, coding became the focus for reimbursement under the diagnosis-related group (DRG) system. Driven by DRG assignment and reimbursement, the quality of coding was forced to be subservient to "optimal" coding in many cases. Now, the financial pendulum is swinging once again to documentation-based coding. Whatever your internal facility's philosophy has been, compliance has shifted the focus to "correct coding for correct reimbursement."

From the coding function, quality and content of documentation naturally flows as the next focus. The documentation function is actually the first function that should be addressed—during the patient's stay. The reason for this is that documentation of the patient's treatment and care is the basis for coding. And, coding is the basis for reimbursement. Without accurate documentation of the patient's condition and treatment, all activities that flow from them are incorrect.

Completeness of documentation (e.g., signatures, transcription), ROI, and record retention were three areas of significant focus for the HIM professional long before compliance was a term in the healthcare provider's vocabulary. These are areas in which written policies and procedures and ensuring that the facility is adhering to laws and regulations have always been the norm.

Now, however, to adhere to a formal compliance program, the HIM department must document the monitoring and education processes for individuals involved in the completeness of documentation, ROI, and record retention functions. What prospective payment did for the coding professional, compliance should do for the rest of the department. Prospective payment elevated the importance of coding by making it the basis for Medicare reimbursement. Compliance, with its emphasis on documentation, record completion, and record retention (as well as coding), has the potential to elevate the importance of *all* functions in the HIM department.

Structure of the team

Once you decide who will be on your team, it's time to think about its size and structure. The size of your compliance team is determined by the size of your department, the number of individuals with expertise in the areas of risk, and your budget. Your team should reflect
- the typical tenets of leadership;
- the typical tenets of strong communication; and
- the culture of your facility and your department.

These three components are equally important to ensure that your team can communicate and cooperate in compliance activities. They also ensure that the team's activities are embraced by other departments, physicians, and other clinicians whose cooperation is essential for HIM compliance throughout your facility.

Get on track—and stay there

Your team should meet regularly in the beginning phases of the compliance planning process. The compliance manager needs to develop clear time frames in which to complete specific activities. You can use the steps in this book as guidelines.

The discussion at each meeting should tie closely to the HIM risk areas and focus on how to minimize that risk. Exhibit 2.2 contains a sample compliance team meeting agenda that you can follow in your own department to help you decide what you need to accomplish. For each meeting, remember to do the following:
- take copious and objective minutes of the meeting;
- have each person present sign an attendance sheet; and
- store all documentation of the meeting safely.

Your team needs to remain focused, focused, *focused!* It needs to accomplish a lot to establish the compliance planning process in an effective and efficient manner. In addition, the team should have a good sense of when to make definitive decisions and when to seek additional input. You need to set benchmarks for accomplishing each task as early as possible. You will determine many of these benchmarks during the assessment and risk identification process (discussed in Step 4).

Exhibit 2.2

HIM Compliance Team Agenda

Staff invited: _____
Date: _____

I. **Designation of HIM compliance manager**
   A. The duties and responsibilities of an HIM compliance manager (see Exhibit 2.1)
   B. Involvement of all HIM management in compliance activities

II. **HIM compliance education**
   A. Deciding what to provide for each HIM employee
   B. Our expectations for each employee regarding HIM compliance
   C. Testing employees' knowledge

III. **Compliance monitoring**
   A. Functions to be monitored
   B. How to conduct the monitoring
   C. Prioritizing the monitoring

IV. **Compliance auditing**
   A. Selecting the right outside firm—determining the criteria
   B. Deciding which functions should be audited

V. **Set a time for the next meeting**

Communication is the key to compliance

In its *Compliance Program Guidance,* the OIG addresses the importance of communication skills. Everyone in your department must know his or her role in the compliance process. Never underestimate the power in numbers. While your compliance team leads the HIM compliance initiative, your department employees hold the key to ensuring that HIM compliance is a success within your facility as whole. Compliance planning in a vacuum has no value; to foster an environment of complete compliance, you must tell others about the compliance activities you're undertaking—not only within your department, but with related departments as well. As a result, your compliance team must develop a good process for communicating within the HIM department and with other relevant staff.

Your team needs to design a process for the flow of communication and ensure that all involved employees understand it. In particular, you need a communication flow that helps you effectively address issues and problems that might arise when designing your compliance program. For example, pay particular attention to other departments that conduct traditional HIM functions. Patient accounting, laboratory, radiology, and other ancillary departments are often responsible for some form of coding. These other departments often call HIM staff on the phone to ask for coding advice. This is a very dangerous practice and can often result in misassigned codes.

If this occurs in your facility, it's important for the HIM department to oversee all of these coding functions to some degree. It's best if all coding functions are pooled together under the HIM umbrella. But if this is not possible, then the HIM department should at least design a communications process between each department involved in coding and the HIM coding staff.

This helps to ensure that the coding is appropriate the first time codes are assigned. You should illustrate this communications loop with a flow chart to help everyone understand it. See Exhibit 2.3 for a sample communications flowchart.

Employees need to know
- what information is important from a compliance perspective; and
- what to do with any important information to which they become privy.

You must ensure that everyone in your department (as well as organization-wide) knows that any communication from a fiscal intermediary (FI) regarding a billing or coding issue is "priority one" from a compliance perspective. Anyone who receives any form of communication from an FI regarding billing or coding issues should not only forward the information to their superior, but also ensure that it is in your "compliance communication loop." For more on the communication process, see **Step 3**—particularly Exhibits 3.6, "Reporting Responsibilities for All Employees" (page 58) and Exhibit 3.7, "Reporting Requirements for All Employees" (page 59).

Audit the communication flow

Once your compliance program is in place, check to make sure that your "communication loop" is still effective in light of new processes. The compliance committee should audit the communication flow chart at least once a year to ensure that it remains effective.

This communication audit should include not only a functional audit, but also interviews with individuals who are in the communication loop. You might want to design a communication audit survey or quiz for staff in all compliance-related departments. The survey should elicit staff members' feelings on the communication

Exhibit 2.3

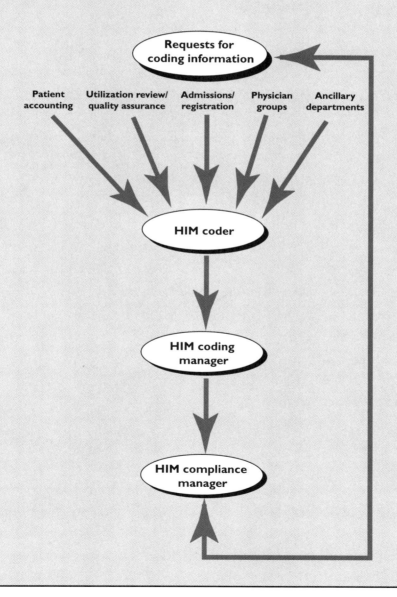

process and their knowledge as to whom they should report potentially noncompliant behavior. The survey should also include questions designed to gain feedback from those who have used the communication loop. The survey should be quick and easy for staff members to complete; this will ensure a high response rate and make it easy to tally results. For a sample survey, see Exhibit 2.4.

Adjusting to compliance

It is important to keep in mind that compliance means some sort of change for almost all of your staff members. As a good manager, you know that most staff members need assistance to adjust to that change. You can help them by engaging each of your staff members as partners in the compliance planning process. Educate them early and teach them to embrace the concept of compliance in all of their responsibilities.

Remind your staff that compliance is a positive change; it results in the elevation of the HIM profession. Explain to them that their jobs have become even more important as a result of compliance and that this is their chance to shine. They'll have the opportunity to help other departments understand compliance and why it is so important to all healthcare providers. You should have little difficulty getting your staff excited about it!

Compliance team review

Here's a summary of what you learned in this step:

- Your HIM compliance team members must have the appropriate skills, values, and personality to lead your compliance effort.

- Your compliance team should include members who have expertise in all areas of HIM compliance risk—including quality and

Exhibit 2.4

HIM Compliance Program Employee Communication Survey

This survey was designed to determine the effectiveness of the HIM department's communication efforts regarding our compliance program.

1. What are the HIM standards of conduct? _____

2. What is your understanding of the government initiative to reduce fraud and abuse in relation to the Medicare and Medicaid regulatory guidelines? _____

3. What measures has our organization—especially the HIM department—taken to reduce potential fraud and abuse? _____

4. Who is on the HIM compliance team? _____

5. Who is the HIM compliance manager? _____

6. Have you read the HIM compliance plan? _____

7. What actions would you take if you encountered another employee acting in violation of the compliance plan or in violation of government regulatory guidelines? _____

8. Have you participated in our HIM compliance education program? What are your current position (i.e., physician, coder, biller, etc.) and your annual education requirements? _____

9. What is our disciplinary policy as it applies to fraudulent behavior? _____

Exhibit 2.4 *continued*

HIM Compliance Program Employee Communication Survey

10. What action would you take if you were approached by a federal or state agent who wants to speak to you about our organization or search an organizational facility? _____
_____

11. Which of the following would you consider to be fraudulent behavior under the federal False Claims Act? Please check yes or no.

    a. Intentionally submitting false records to
       receive government payments.   ❏ Yes ❏ No
    b. Unintentionally billing laboratory services separately
       when they should be combined or bundled.   ❏ Yes ❏ No
    c. Altering clinical documentation in order to increase
       reimbursement for the organization.   ❏ Yes ❏ No

12. Please read the following scenarios. Which contain fraudulent behavior?

    Scenario I: Dr. Jones is a well-known, respected physician in the community. As a courtesy to her patients, it is her practice to waive Medicare copayments and deductibles and bill only Medicare for the services provided. Is this fraudulent behavior?   ❏ Yes ❏ No

    Scenario II: A physician failed to provide a diagnosis on a patient who needs laboratory services. Sarah, who has worked in the lab for many years, paged the treating physician to request that a diagnosis be faxed to the lab. Despite her diligent efforts, the physician did not respond. Sarah reviewed the requested test and coded a diagnosis that she believed to be appropriate, given her many years of experience. She then submitted the claim to billing. Is this fraudulent behavior?   ❏ Yes ❏ No

    Scenario III: Hospital A has an excellent relationship with its medical staff. To show its appreciation for the great work that the physicians do, the administration frequently provides them with $10 gift certificates to a nearby restaurant. Is this fraudulent behavior?   ❏ Yes ❏ No

Reprinted with permission from QuadraMed Corporation. Copyright 1998.

content of documentation, completeness of documentation, coding and abstracting, ROI, and record retention.

- The structure of your team should reflect not only necessary skill sets, but also the culture of your institution.

- Weave communication into the fabric of your compliance program, focusing on those departments that perform traditional HIM functions—especially coding.

- Every HIM staff member must recognize his or her responsibility for compliance; your compliance team is only the first line of defense.

— STEP 3 —

Developing Your Standards of Conduct

— STEP 3 —

Developing Your Standards of Conduct

"A written guide that describes the organization's philosophy of doing business"

In a nutshell, that's the definition of a document known in the compliance world as the "standards of conduct." Writing this guide is the first step in not only the organization's compliance planning process, but also that of your health information management (HIM) department. First, however, you need to understand what goes into the standards of conduct, whether for your entire organization or for your HIM department.

What exactly are standards of conduct?

Some people see the standards of conduct statement as a glorified version of the mission and vision statements. While it's true that the mission and vision statements are part of the standards of conduct, there's much more to it than that. The standards should outline in detail how laws, regulations, guidelines, and accreditation standards guide the way an organization conducts business. The standards need to address how these laws and regulations affect each employee in performing his or her job. Plus, they should provide the steps an employee takes if he or she is aware of any potentially noncompliant activity.

The standards of conduct statement is a written document that staff members read during orientation and keep with them as a reference throughout their employment with the organization. For a list of what the standards of conduct should contain, see Exhibit 3.1.

Before writing the standards, an organization needs to have a true understanding of its culture. "Culture" is defined as an organization's values. Once an organization identifies those values, it can translate them into principles that govern its business conduct—principles that are at the core of the organization—and encourage all staff members to comply. It is very important that the standards of conduct reflect the corporate culture, rather than being a boilerplate document that is simply borrowed from another organization or a consultant. Employees can easily spot standards that don't fit the organization. But if they do fit, employees will take the standards seriously and follow them.

Standards of conduct documents should change only when a major event occurs. For example, organizations that merge or acquire other groups will need to modify standards of conduct to reflect these kinds of changes. Changes in the laws that govern

Exhibit 3.1

Contents of the Standards of Conduct

An organization's standards of conduct should contain the following:

- Mission, vision, philosophy, core values, or similar corporate statements.

- A statement that reflects the organization's philosophy on conducting business legally, ethically, and fairly.

- An explanation of how laws, regulations, guidelines, and accreditation standards affect the way the organization conducts business.

- Examples of how these laws and regulations affect employees' daily activities.

- Steps that employees should take if they detect potentially noncompliant behavior.

the healthcare industry might also require standards to adjust. In general, however, an organization's standards of conduct statement needs to be an enduring document that reflects the way all employees should conduct business.

HIM standards of conduct

The corporate standards of conduct should address some or all HIM functions, but not to the extent that you discuss them in your department's standards. As stated above, it's important to have standards of conduct that are specific to the HIM department because so many HIM activities can place the facility at risk of noncompliance. You should address each of these activities individually in the HIM standards. Include examples that are specific to HIM staff and make references to specific HIM department policies and procedures.

The HIM department standards of conduct should reference and complement the corporate standards of conduct, as well as mirror their general flavor. Compliance is a concept to embrace in a uniform manner throughout the organization. You want to reflect this idea in the HIM standards of conduct. Also, it's important to be consistent with the corporate standards as you address each of your department functions.

If your organization has not yet developed a corporate standards of conduct, that shouldn't stop you from developing HIM-specific standards. Take the lead with your own department while you encourage your organization to develop corporate-wide standards. Inform the corporate compliance staff of your intention to develop HIM standards. Tell them that you will be prepared not only to share the results with them, but also to have the group use your standards as a model for the HIM risk pieces that are addressed in the corporate compliance standards.

You then want to try to make sure you have HIM department representation on the committee that develops the corporate-wide standards of conduct.

Content of HIM standards of conduct

Once you make the commitment to develop standards of conduct for your department, you need to decide on the contents of this document. While you want to tailor your standards to the unique needs of your own department, in general, HIM standards should contain these items:
- a statement of ethics;
- general references to laws, regulations, and accreditation standards that guide the work of staff in the following functional areas:
    - content and quality of documentation;
    - completeness of documentation;
    - coding and abstracting;
    - release of information (ROI);
    - record retention and storage;
- examples of how the laws and regulations affect HIM employees in their everyday job duties; and
- lines of communication within the department, as well as with other departments, to report potential noncompliance.

Developing your statement of ethics

The statement of ethics sets the stage for the HIM standards of conduct. As you put forth your own department's statement of ethics, you should also discuss the ethics of the HIM profession as a whole. Here, you could include the American Health Information Management Association's (AHIMA) *Code of Ethics and Bylaws* (see the Preamble in Exhibit 3.2). All HIM department employees should understand the *Code of Ethics* and follow it in their daily job functions. The 10 principles are basic, but intrinsic to everyday HIM operations.

Exhibit 3.2

Preamble to AHIMA's Code of Ethics and Bylaws

The Health Information Management Professional abides by a set of ethical principles developed to safeguard the public and to contribute within the scope of the profession to quality and efficiency in health care. This Code of Ethics, adopted by the members of the American Health Information Management Association, defines the standards of behavior which promote ethical conduct.

I. The Health Information Management Professional demonstrates behavior that reflects integrity, supports objectivity, and fosters trust in professional activities.

II. The Health Information Management Professional respects the dignity of each human being.

III. The Health Information Management Professional strives to improve personal competence and quality of services.

IV. The Health Information Management Professional represents truthfully and accurately professional credentials, education, and experience.

V. The Health Information Management Professional refuses to participate in illegal or unethical acts and also refuses to conceal the illegal, incompetent, or unethical acts of others.

VI. The Health Information Management Professional protects the confidentiality of primary and secondary health records as mandated by law, professional standards, and the employer's policies.

VII. The Health Information Management Professional promotes to others the tenets of confidentiality.

VIII. The Health Information Management Professional adheres to pertinent laws and regulations while advocating changes which serve the best interest of the public.

Exhibit 3.2 *continued*

> **Preamble to AHIMA's Code of Ethics and Bylaws**
>
> IX. The Health Information Management Professional encourages appropriate use of health record information and advocates policies and systems that advance the management of health records and health information.
>
> X. The Health Information Management Professional recognizes and supports the Association's mission.
>
> Reprinted with permission from the American Health Information Management Association (AHIMA). Bylaws amended October 1997, Code of Ethics amended 1993.

In the section on professional ethics, you should also address the basic tenet of confidentiality of patient information. AHIMA's *Code of Ethics* addresses this topic, so again, you can point to this document as a reference. Explain in your standards how your facility and your department embrace this important concept.

You should also refer to AHIMA's coding standards in the ethics section of your standards of conduct (see Exhibit 3.3). AHIMA's *Standards of Ethical Coding* focus on the tenets of coding and abstracting. You should reference these guidelines here and use them as the basis for the coding section as well. In addition, you can refer to AHIMA's *Certified Coding Specialist (CCS) Competencies* and *Certified Coding Specialist—Physician-Based (CCS-P) Competencies* as resources for your coding standards (see Exhibits 3.4 and 3.5).

Referring to laws and standards

In the second section of your standards of conduct, you need to reference the laws that govern each area of compliance risk in an HIM department.

Exhibit 3.3

AHIMA's Standards of Ethical Coding

These standards were developed by the American Health Information Management Association (AHIMA) Council on Coding and Classification to give medical coders ethical guidelines for performing their tasks. They are intended to impart the responsibility and importance coders have as members of the healthcare team and to support them as dignified professionals.

In this era of payment based on diagnostic and procedural coding, the professional ethics of medical record coders continue to be challenged. The following standards of ethical coding developed by the AHIMA Council on Coding and Classification and approved by the AHIMA Board of Directors are offered to guide the coder in this process.*

I. Diagnoses that are present on admission or diagnoses and procedures that occur during the current encounter are to be abstracted after a thorough review of the entire medical record. Those diagnoses not applicable to the current encounter should not be abstracted.

II. Selection of the principal diagnosis and principal procedure, along with other diagnoses and procedures, must meet the definitions of the Uniform Hospital Discharge Data Set (UHDDS).

III. Assessment must be made of the documentation in the chart to ensure that it is adequate and appropriate to support he diagnoses and procedures selected to be abstracted.

IV. Medical record coders should use their skills, their knowledge of ICD-9-CM and CPT, and any available resources to select diagnostic and procedural codes.

V. Medical record coders should not change codes or narratives of codes that the meanings are misrepresented. Nor should diagnoses or procedures be included or excluded because the payment will be affected. Statistical clinical data is an important result of coding, and maintaining a quality database should be a conscientious goal.

VI. Physicians should be consulted for clarification when they enter conflicting or ambiguous documentation in the chart.

Exhibit 3.3 *continued*

> ### AHIMA's Standards of Ethical Coding
>
> VII. The medical record coder is a member of the healthcare team and, as such, should assist physicians who are unfamiliar with ICD-9-CM, CPT, or DRG methodology by suggesting resequencing or inclusion of diagnoses or procedures when needed to more accurately reflect the occurrence of events during the encounter.
>
> VIII. The medical record coder is expected to strive for the optimal payment to which the facility is legally entitled, but it is unethical and illegal to maximize payment by means that contradict regulatory guidelines.
>
> *The Official Coding Guidelines, published by the Cooperating Parties (American Hospital Association, American Health Information Management Association, Health Care Financing Administration, and National Center for Health Statistics), should be followed in all facilities regardless of payment source.
>
> *Reprinted with permission from the American Health Information Management Association (AHIMA).*

Content and quality of documentation

The content and quality of documentation is governed primarily by the Medicare Conditions of Participation and Health Care Financing Administration (HCFA) administrative regulations. Make reference in your standards of conduct to the need to ensure that documentation sufficiently addresses the issue of medical necessity. Medical necessity is particularly important from a compliance perspective; the lack of sufficient documentation to support medical necessity will result in a denial of payment for a claim. The concept of content and quality of documentation, as well as the determination of medical necessity, can be very subjective. That is why it is important to stress the importance of documentation quality. It could mean the difference between claim denial or payment. If Medicare determines that the claims are the result of a "pattern or practice," it could mean significant False Claims Act exposure.

Step 3: Developing Your Standards of Conduct

Exhibit 3.4

AHIMA's CCS Coding Competencies

Hospital-based competencies

A. Data identification
1. Read and interpret health record documentation to identify all diagnoses and procedures that affect the current inpatient stay/outpatient encounter visit

2. Assess the adequacy of health record documentation to ensure that it supports all diagnoses and procedures to which codes are assigned

3. Apply knowledge of anatomy and physiology, clinical disease processes, pharmacology, and diagnostic and procedural terminology to assign accurate codes to diagnoses and procedures

4. Apply knowledge of disease processes and surgical procedures to assign nonindexed medical terms to the appropriate class in the classification/nomenclature system

B. Coding guidelines
1. Apply knowledge of current approved "ICD-9-CM Coding and Reporting Official Guidelines"* to assign and sequence the correct diagnosis and procedure codes for hospital inpatient services

2. Apply knowledge of current "Diagnostic Coding and Reporting Guidelines for Outpatient Services"*

3. Apply knowledge of CPT format, guidelines, and notes to locate the correct codes for all services and procedures performed during the encounter/visit and sequence them correctly

4. Apply knowledge of procedural terminology to recognize when an unlisted procedure code must be used in CPT

C. Regulatory guidelines
1. Apply Uniform Hospital Discharge Data Set (UHDDS) definitions to select the principal diagnosis, principal procedure, complications and comorbid conditions, other diagnoses and significant procedures which require coding

47

Exhibit 3.4 *continued*

AHIMA's CCS Coding Competencies

2. Select the appropriate principal diagnosis for episodes of care in which determination of principal diagnosis is not clear because the patient has multiple problems

3. Apply knowledge of the Prospective Payment System to confirm DRG assignment which ensures optimal reimbursement

4. Refuse to fraudulently maximize reimbursement by assigning codes that do not conform to approved coding principles/guidelines*

5. Refuse to unfairly maximize reimbursement by unbundling services and codes that do not conform to CPT basic coding principles

6. Apply knowledge of the Ambulatory Surgery Center (ASC) Payment Groups to confirm ASC assignment which ensures optimal reimbursement

7. Apply policies and procedures on health record documentation, coding, and claims processing and appeal

8. Use the HCFA Common Procedural Coding System (HCPCS) to appropriately assign HCPCS codes for outpatient Medicare reimbursement

D. Coding
1. Exclude from coding diagnoses, conditions, problems, and procedures related to an earlier episode of care which have no bearing on the current episode of care

2. Exclude from coding ICD-9-CM nonsurgical, noninvasive procedures which carry no operative or anesthetic risk

3. Exclude from coding information such as symptoms or signs characteristic of the diagnosis, findings from diagnostic studies, or localized conditions, which have no bearing on the current management of the patient

4. Apply knowledge of ICD-9-CM instructional notations and conventions to locate and assign the correct diagnosis and procedural codes and sequence them correctly

Exhibit 3.4 *continued*

AHIMA's CCS Coding Competencies

5. Facilitate data retrieval by recognizing when more than one code is required to adequately classify a given condition

6. Exclude from coding those procedures which are component parts of an already assigned CPT procedure code

E. Data quality
1. Clarify conflicting, ambiguous, or nonspecific information appearing in a health record by consulting the appropriate physician

2. Participate in quality assessment to ensure continuous improvement in ICD-9-CM and CPT coding and collection of quality health data

3. Demonstrate ability to recognize potential coding quality issues from an array of data

4. Apply policies and procedures on health record documentation and coding that are consistent with official coding guidelines*

5. Contribute to development of facility-specific coding policies and procedures

*The cooperating parties (American Health Information Management Association, American Hospital Association, Health Care Financing Administration, National Center for Health Statistics) publish official guidelines in the *Coding Clinic for ICD-9-CM*, available from the American Hospital Association. These guidelines are also available in the ICD-9-CM CD-ROM offered by the US Government Printing Office. "ICD-9-CM Coding and Reporting Official Guidelines" and "Diagnostic Coding and Reporting Guidelines for Outpatient Services (Hospital-Based and Physician Offices)" published in Fourth Quarter, 1995, *Coding Clinic for ICD-9-CM* (Volume 7, No. 1).

The CPT Assistant newsletter, published by the American Medical Association, is also considered a coding resource for the CCS exam.

Reprinted with permission from the American Health Information Management Association (AHIMA).

Exhibit 3.5

AHIMA's CCS-P Coding Competencies (July 1998)

Physician-based competencies

A. Data identification
1. Read and interpret visit documentation to identify codeable diagnoses and procedures for data capture and billing

2. Read and interpret medical record documentation to identify all diagnoses, conditions, problems, or other reasons for the outpatient encounter and all services and procedures performed during that visit

3. Assess the adequacy of medical record documentation to ensure that it supports the codes assigned

4. Apply knowledge of disease processes to assign codes to conditions/medical terms not found in the index of the coding book to the appropriate class in the classification system

B. Coding guidelines
1. Understand the use and function of modifiers in CPT

2. Apply the "ICD-9-CM Coding Guidelines for Outpatient Services"* and knowledge of instructional notations and conventions to select and sequence diagnoses, conditions, problems, or other reasons which require coding

3. Apply knowledge of CPT guidelines, format, and notes to locate and correctly sequence codes for all services and procedures performed during the encounter

4. Confirm Evaluation and Management (E/M) codes based upon medical record documentation using the E/M guidelines

5. Recognize when an unlisted code must be used

6. Demonstrate ability to recognize potential coding quality issues from an array of data (e.g., explanation of benefits, coding databases, etc.)

Step 3: Developing Your Standards of Conduct

Exhibit 3.5 *continued*

AHIMA's CCS-P Coding Competencies (July 1998)

C. Regulatory guidelines
1. Apply regulatory agency guidelines (i.e., HCFA) to coding principles so that codes are assigned correctly to each visit

2. Observe guidelines on bundling and unbundling

3. Have knowledge of the global surgical package and its components

4. Have knowledge of various reimbursement methodologies, fee schedule, and RBRVS

5. Execute policies and procedures on medical record documentation, coding, claims filing, and claims appeal

D. Coding
1. Exclude from coding those procedures which are component parts of an already assigned procedure code

2. Assign Level II HCPCS codes correctly for services not found in CPT (e.g., administration of drugs, durable medical equipment)

3. Attach modifiers to procedure or service codes when applicable

4. Appropriately code for the professional vs. technical competent when applicable

5. Assign ICD-9-CM code(s) for conditions managed or treated during the encounter

6. Assign CPT code(s) for procedures and/or services rendered during the encounter

7. Evaluate the disease processes as related to various ancillary procedures

E. Data quality
1. Query physicians when additional information is needed for coding and/or to clarify conflicting or ambiguous information

Exhibit 3.5 *continued*

> ### AHIMA's CCS-P Coding Competencies (July 1998)
>
> 2. Link ICD-9-CM code(s) to proper CPT code(s) to ensure accurate claims submission
>
> 3. Verify that the CPT code(s), ICD-9-CM code(s), and Place of Service code(s) on the HCFA 1500 claim form correctly support the services performed
>
> 4. Determine educational needs for physicians and staff on coding, reimbursement, and documentation rules as well as penalties and sanction possibilities (e.g., standardized encounter form/progress notes)
>
> *The cooperating parties (American Health Information Management Association, American Hospital Association, Health Care Financing Administration, National Center for Health Statistics) publish official guidelines in the *Coding Clinic for ICD-9-CM*, available from the American Hospital Association. These guidelines are also available in the ICD-9-CM CD-ROM offered by the US Government Printing Office. "ICD-9-CM Coding and Reporting Official Guidelines" and "Diagnostic Coding and Reporting Guidelines for Outpatient Services (Hospital-Based and Physician Offices)" published in Fourth Quarter, 1995, *Coding Clinic for ICD-9-CM* (Volume 7, No. 1).

Reprinted with permission from the American Health Information Management Association (AHIMA).

Completeness of documentation

An incomplete patient record puts the entire organization at a high risk both legally and in terms of compliance. The HIM department's responsibility is paramount in this area. In this section of the standards, it is important to discuss the department's goals for ensuring that records are complete. Your standards should include references to the content of the patient record as well as amending or correcting entries.

The Office of the Inspector General's (OIG) *Compliance Program Guidance for Hospitals* references these types of documentation issues that should be addressed generally in the standards and

Step 3: Developing Your Standards of Conduct

specifically through departmental policies and procedures:
- billing necessity (billing only for documented services);
- medical necessity;
- correct coding;
- outpatient services rendered in connection with inpatient stays (72-hour rule, now referred to as the three-day window);
- patient transfers;
- credit balances;
- laboratory compliance; and
- record retention.

Completeness of the patient record is governed by the Medicare Conditions of Participation, state licensure requirements, and Joint Commission on Accreditation of Healthcare Organization (JCAHO) standards. Refer to each of these regulations and guidelines in your standards of conduct. You also need to refer to internal guidelines, such as your organization's medical staff bylaws, that probably include sanctions for physicians who don't complete records in a timely manner. In addition, you should point to the HIM department's policies and procedures as a guide to help employees perform their job duties correctly.

Coding and abstracting

HIM standards need to provide details on coding and abstracting functions. The government is currently focused on the process of coding and abstracting. You might want to emphasize this area in your standards of conduct and provide even more information on how to maintain compliance while performing these duties.

The OIG's *Compliance Program Guidance* lists several HIM functions that facilities should include in their organizational standards. They include
- complete documentation;

- correct coding and diagnosis-related group (DRG) assignment; and
- documentation-based reimbursement.

Although the government is now focused on inpatient coding and DRG assignments, you must address all types of coding in your standards. Rules for ICD-9-CM inpatient coding are provided by HCFA directives (often interpreted and handed down by fiscal intermediaries [FI]) and the American Hospital Association's (AHA) *Coding Clinic for ICD-9-CM*. Your standards should point out that the coding staff follows the official advice and guidance that these resources provide.

Your standards should also state the importance of documenting all communications with HCFA and your FI. This documentation should preserve the questions your department asks and the answers that HCFA and the intermediary provide. It's also important for the plan to provide guidance to coding staff regarding coding issues that are not addressed by HCFA or official guidelines. Your department should have a specific protocol for coders to follow in these cases to ensure accurate and consistent coding.

In most cases, the coding supervisor is the first line of defense; coders should be able to turn to their supervisor for answers. But there are times when the coding supervisor needs additional guidance. The standards should detail where the coding supervisor can turn to for help within the facility.

The Uniform Hospital Discharge Data Set (UHDDS) governs the abstracting process. UHDDS specifies which data elements are abstracted and defines each data item. This ensures consistency in the reporting of data elements throughout the country. Your staff must know where they can access the data element definitions of UHDDS. You could include this information in your standards of conduct as a reference.

Refer to your facility's policies and procedures for coding and abstracting; staff members need to know where they can go within the department to get more details. Remember that you should reference the department policies and procedures in your standards, but not reprint them there. The primary purpose of the standards is to serve as a guide and general reference tool for the employee.

Release of information

When we discussed ethics earlier (page 44), we addressed confidentiality of patient information. Since healthcare was first institutionalized, patient confidentiality has been an important issue. ROI is governed by federal and state laws as well as Medicare's Conditions of Participation and JCAHO standards.

In the last decade, new federal—as well as many state—laws have addressed the highly sensitive nature of certain patient documentation. These include laws on substance abuse, psychiatric, and HIV-infected patients. They require that the documentation of these types of patients receive special care to protect their confidentiality. The fact that the federal government has acknowledged the significance of these special types of patient records makes their protection by the HIM professional even more important. That's why it's important to reference these laws in your standards of conduct.

Your standards of conduct should address the general requirements for a valid ROI as well as those limited instances when information should not be released. Valid reasons for ROI include
- "nonpersonal" use of the record in research and education;
- medical care evaluation;
- patient care; and
- a required release by law (i.e., valid subpoena).

Record retention and storage

In recent years, record retention has taken on a more significant role in compliance and legal issues. Many court cases have been settled against providers who were unable to locate patient records. Court findings often favor the plaintiff in the absence of documentation—regardless of the circumstantial evidence. Therefore, the inability to locate patient records places the facility at a high risk of legal exposure, and consequently, noncompliance.

Your standards of conduct should emphasize the importance of retrievability of records, as well as the way you store your records (e.g., microfilm, optical disk imaging, off-site storage). We often take for granted the ability to find records, but you need to stress the significance of that function to all employees. The standards of conduct is a good place to do just that.

Each state has its own laws regarding the retention of records. Usually, age of majority plus the statute of limitations for malpractice are the minimum time for retention. These laws were generally passed based upon the amount of time a patient has to bring a lawsuit against a facility. Now, because of the new application of the False Claims Act to billing and coding functions, it is necessary to take another look at record retention. Generally, claims can be brought under the False Claims Act up to seven years after the incident. However, on occasion, the time has been extended to 10 years. Therefore, you should set a policy of retaining medical records for at least 10 years.

Reporting possible noncompliance

If an employee spots what he or she believes is noncompliance, the last thing you want that employee to do is to become a "whistleblower" and take that information to the government.

Step 3: Developing Your Standards of Conduct

You need to have a procedure for reporting such information internally—and you need to make sure your employees understand that procedure. Employees need to understand what their roles in the compliance process are (see Exhibit 3.6). You should also provide guidelines detailing the channels of communication employees should follow to report the information. You might want to put this information in a diagram format to help your staff understand the process more clearly (see Exhibit 3.7).

You must assure your employees that they do not have to fear retribution if they report potentially noncompliant activity. A good way to allay those fears and to encourage reporting is to set up a hotline, which allows for anonymous reporting. If your organization has already decided how to approach the use of hotlines, your standards should reflect the corporate policy. Your standards should also reflect reporting guidelines that have been published and disseminated to all staff.

You need to educate staff about how to determine if an act is potentially noncompliant. Let them know what types of activity are appropriate to report to the hotline and what are not. Some activities, such as releasing patient records without the proper authorization, are easy to categorize as noncompliant. Other activities, however, are in a "gray" area.

For example, if a staff member uses "unofficial" resources for coding advice or files incomplete records in the "complete file" area, you should document the unacceptable nature of this type of conduct. But in each of these cases, there could be extenuating circumstances. In the case of coding, there are situations that official guidelines do not address. If the coder uses unofficial resources in such a situation, then whether there was a violation would depend on the resource used and the written policy in place for coders in

Exhibit 3.6

Reporting Responsibilities for All Employees

Employees
A corporation is built by its individual employees. As such, the conduct, judgment, and decision-making of every employee are the largest and most important driving factors that determine its regulatory compliance, corporate integrity, and business ethics. We rely on each other to do what is right. Day to day we must strive to ensure integrity in all of our interactions with colleagues, clients, suppliers, and competitors. Likewise, each of us needs to report any suspected violations of this code or accepted standards of ethical business practices.

Managers
Managers must strive to set a good example of integrity and ethical behavior. They must be very careful not to place pressure on employees to violate our standards of conduct in any way. Further, managers must be receptive and responsive to any compliance-related or corporate integrity issue brought to their attention. Managers are responsible for reporting all possible violations of which they are aware to the compliance officer.

Human resources
The human resources department is available to assist all employees with a wide range of compliance issues and problems. Although you should first speak with your manager regarding integrity issues, employees can discuss these issues with human resources, if necessary. Like managers, human resources staff are responsible for reporting potential violations to the compliance officer.

Compliance officer
The compliance officer serves our employees in several ways. He or she examines policies and procedures for real-world applications. The cornerstone of the compliance officer's efforts is communication. Through updates, education, and routine communication, the compliance officer keeps employees informed as to what is expected of them in the compliance process. Employees can contact the compliance officer anonymously or in confidence to ask questions or to voice concerns.

Reprinted with permission from QuadraMed Corporation. Copyright 1998.

Step 3: Developing Your Standards of Conduct

Exhibit 3.7

Reporting Requirements for All Employees

As an employee of our organization, you are responsible for your ethical behavior. You are also responsible for promptly reporting possible violations to the appropriate channels. Managers and supervisors must be careful in both words and conduct to avoid placing, or appearing to place, pressure on subordinates that could cause them to violate these standards of conduct or to deviate from accepted norms of ethical business practices.

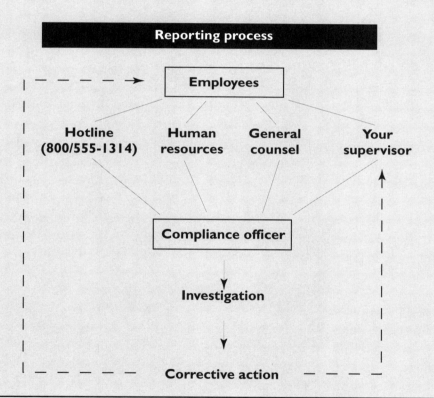

Remember: Employees are the key component in the compliance reporting cascade. Each individual employee is the first and best assurance of compliance integrity and business ethics. Therefore, you are personally responsible for interfacing with your manager, the human resources department, the compliance hotline, and the compliance officer to report suspected code of conduct violations and resolve any compliance questions and issues that you encounter in your day-to-day activities.

Reprinted with permission from QuadraMed Corporation. Copyright 1998.

these predicaments. In the other example, incomplete records filed in the complete area might occur in the case of a deceased physician. You would need to address the specifics in light of department policies and procedures for this situation.

If left without further instruction, employees could potentially report a plethora of gray area activities. Provide staff with as much information as possible via the standards and educational sessions to allow staff to assess a situation and make the right decision about whether or not to report it.

Include real-life examples in HIM standards
Including real-life examples in your HIM standards serves several purposes:

- Examples make the standards "real" to the staff and encourage a greater degree of support for them.

- They allow for greater understanding of all standards, especially those with which a particular employee might not have much experience.

- Real-life examples help employees decide if behavior is noncompliant.

You should describe at least two scenarios for every HIM function you address in the standards (i.e., content and quality of documentation, completeness of documentation, coding and abstracting, ROI, and record retention and storage). Derive your examples from activities that take place in your own department. The more realistic they are, the more effective they are. We have included several possible scenarios in Exhibit 3.8.

Exhibit 3.8

Real-life Scenarios for the Standards of Conduct

Scenario I: Content, quality, and completeness of documentation
Situation: While reviewing a patient record on the floor for concurrent coding, you notice that the physician has documented a diagnosis of "gram negative pneumonia" on the facesheet. However, there is no evidence in the progress notes, culture and sensitivity, lab tests, or other documentation located in the body of the record to support the fact that the patient has gram negative pneumonia. What should you do?

Action: At a minimum, bring this lack of documentation to the physician's attention, explaining the need to either change the diagnosis or append the documentation in the patient's record to reflect the patient's actual condition. Depending on your internal policies, report this information to a clinical department and/or a compliance specialist. Document this occurrence, along with the physician's response to your question, and file it with other relevant compliance documentation. You should make this occurrence a part of your compliance monitoring report for the time period as well.

Scenario II: Coding and abstracting
Situation: Your department has brought in a consulting/education firm to perform a coding audit. During the follow-up education session, the presenter (a representative from this firm) states that, in the absence of documentation to the contrary, staff should code all bacterial pneumonia cases to Code 482.89 (other specified bacterial pneumonia). Using this code will ensure that all cases documented as bacterial pneumonia are assigned to the higher-paying pneumonia DRG. You are a participant in this education session. You realize that the recommendation is contrary not only to internal policies, but also to AHA *Coding Clinic* guidelines. What should you do?

Action: You need to immediately intervene to correct the presenter's inaccurate teaching and ensure that no staff members leave that session with misinformation. If a compliance or management representative is present, seek him or her out, explain the issue, and confront the presenter together. If no representative is present, address the issue yourself and correct it with references to your internal policies and official guidelines. Document the information, date, time, and name of the presenter, along with the references to internal policies and AHA Coding Clinic *guidelines. Forward this information to your HIM compliance manager or the facility's compliance officer.*

Scenario III: Release of information
Situation: One of your patients expired in your facility. The patient's sister arrives at

Exhibit 3.8 *continued*

> ### Real-life Scenarios for the Standards of Conduct
>
> your door to request a copy of his medical record. She explains that she has been appointed as the trustee for her brother's estate, producing as proof a copy of a letter from a local attorney. What should you do?
>
> *Action: Explain to the requestor that you can only accept an official document from the probate court appointing her as trustee for her brother's estate. You may not rely on the attorney's letter in this situation.*
>
> **Scenario IV: Record retention and storage**
> Situation: You see a resident stuffing a patient's record in his backpack on his way out of the department. What should you do?
>
> *Action: Confront the resident immediately and explain that under no circumstances are patient records permitted to leave the facility. Cite the applicable standard of conduct and law, if necessary. Request the record back and return it to its appropriate place in the department. Document the entire incident, including the date, time, name of the resident, your name, and the patient record number and name, and give this information to your HIM compliance manager.*

Educating staff on the standards of conduct

It's your responsibility to "sell" the standards of conduct to your staff. You must ensure that staff read, understand, and keep the standards fresh in their minds. Employees are more likely to embrace the standards if you can make educational sessions interactive and interesting. For example, you could
- include a short test at the end of a session;
- have small discussion groups address different compliance scenarios;
- invite physicians, ethics professors, or other respected professionals to participate in the presentation; and
- create an interactive computer program that gives employees a chance to solve sample compliance problems.

Step 3: Developing Your Standards of Conduct

As the HIM director, you must demonstrate the importance of the standards through the time and effort you put into them. Set aside time to speak with employees in small groups to impress upon them the significance of the standards. And, you should make sure they know that the standards are just the beginning of the process. In essence, the standards kick off a series of compliance-related activities that will become a permanent part of the HIM department.

Presentation and packaging are important considerations. You expect employees to hold on to this document as a reference tool to guide them throughout their tenures in the department. Consequently, you should provide them with a document that is worth keeping. While substance and content are the primary and critical concerns, the document's format adds to its effectiveness as well. Make your standards of conduct document as elaborate as your budget allows. Here are some examples of what you could do:

- Have your standards of conduct document professionally printed in four-color format with pictures.

- Print them on a laser color printer, import artwork, and bind them in a booklet format.

- Print them on 8 1/2 x 17 parchment paper (available in most office supply stores) and fold into a booklet format.

- Print them on colored paper with unique fonts for the title and other parts that you want to stand out.

- Make them available on your network with imported artwork—only if you have the ability to make the documents permanent so they cannot be changed by those viewing them.

The final stage: signing off

After staff members have read the standards for the first time, you should require them to sign an official document that states that they have read and understand the standards of conduct and that they agree to abide by them. File this signed document in each employee's permanent file. For a sample statement of understanding, see Exhibit 3.9.

You might also want to request that all of your vendors sign off on your standards of conduct as well. Provide each vendor annually

Exhibit 3.9

Employee Statement of Understanding for the Standards of Conduct

Community Hospital

I have completely read and understand Community Hospital's standards of conduct. I agree to follow the policies, procedures, spirit, and tenets presented in this document. I will perform my duties at Community Hospital in compliance with the law and with the highest ethical and moral standards. I will report any known or suspected violations of these standards to the appropriate hospital representatives.

Please fill out this section and submit the entire form to your manager.

Name: _____

Title: _____

Date: _____

Signature: _____

Step 3: Developing Your Standards of Conduct

with a copy of your standards of conduct and your updated policies and procedures. This is an important protection not only for the HIM department, but for the facility in general. All vendors should have their own compliance plans. Having them sign off on yours further emphasizes the importance your facility places on running its business according to the laws, regulations, and guidelines that govern it. You could easily adapt our sample employee sign-off sheet to use for vendors.

Standards of conduct review

Remember to do the following when writing your standards of conduct:

- Address federal and state laws and administrative regulations that govern the functions of content and quality of documentation, completeness of documentation, coding and abstracting, ROI, and record retention.

- Stress the importance of the specific tasks involved in successfully carrying out each of these functions in a legal, ethical, and fair manner.

- Make a general reference to your department policies and procedures that pertain to these functions.

- Educate your staff and your vendors on your standards of conduct, making sure that they have read and understand them.

— STEP 4 —

Conducting a Compliance Assessment

— Step 4 —

Conducting a Compliance Assessment

Once you complete your standards of conduct document, your next step is to conduct a health information management (HIM) compliance assessment. A compliance assessment is similar to an operational assessment in that it analyzes the way that work is done. However, the compliance assessment is also broader; in addition to improving processes, it focuses on identifying potential compliance risk areas. In your assessment, you will use the information from your standards of conduct to focus on the exact steps of these processes that, if not performed correctly, might potentially place the HIM department and your entire organization at compliance risk.

How to conduct a compliance assessment

You need to conduct an initial, or baseline, compliance assessment when you begin to implement your compliance program. Conduct a follow-up assessment every year thereafter to ensure that your department remains compliant. Use these six steps to perform your assessment:

1. Interview staff members who perform the process.

2. Trace the actual steps of the staff members as they perform the process.

3. Create a flow chart to document the process as you witnessed it.

4. Create a flow chart to document the process as you believe it should occur.

5. Analyze the process results.

6. Overlay the flow charts to identify areas of risk.

As you perform your assessment for each of the functions, there are certain issues that should alert you to a potential compliance risk. These risks will formulate the basis for your monitoring activity, which we address in **Step 5.** As a general rule, pay particular attention in the assessment process to these items that might trigger compliance risk:
- an automated or manual step without any oversight, quality assurance (QA), or review;
- the use of any computer system that appears to perform its own edits or other changes to data without any human intervention;
- inconsistencies in the process from one individual to another;
- the use of outside vendors to perform the process; and
- the need to rely heavily (in performing the task) on complex regulations, frequent fiscal intermediary communications, or other complex or voluminous resources such as the American Hospital Association's (AHA) *Coding Clinic*, the *CPT Assistant*, or the *Carrier Manuals*. Much of this information is not accessible electronically and requires detailed analysis to ensure compliance, therefore making it a compliance risk.

Internal versus external assessment
The first line of action is to decide if you should hire an outside firm or use your own staff to conduct the assessment. If you can identify a firm that has both the understanding of the HIM operations process and expertise in the compliance area, you should retain its services. Here are some other reasons to use an external firm:
- an external firm provides an objective, unbiased point of view;
- staff members might be more willing to divulge certain information

Step 4: Conducting a Compliance Assessment

to an external firm that they might not otherwise share with their superior(s);
- an external firm might have certain expertise necessary for the compliance assessment that your facility cannot provide internally; and
- the government or other third party might feel there is more credibility to an outside assessment than one performed internally.

It's good to use an external firm to provide your initial "baseline" compliance assessment at least. Once you have an objective baseline assessment, however, you might find it effective in subsequent years to conduct the follow-up assessments yourself.

If you have a limited budget for the assessment, you might choose to have an external firm review only those functions that you believe contain the highest risk. In most HIM departments, these include the coding and abstracting processes. You could then assess the other functions internally.

Assessment of the content and quality of documentation

The medical record contains documentation for all patient care and treatment. This is true not only for the patient's attending and consulting physicians, but also for all allied health and nursing personnel who have provided any sort of care for the patient. Accurate documentation of patient care is important not only to ensure high quality care and communication among the clinicians treating the patient, but also to act as proof of care for all charges generated for that patient stay.

Documentation issues range from the use of effective forms to ensuring that documentation is complete from clinicians in all areas of the hospital. Because there are so many documentation challenges in the patient record, it is a good idea to focus initially on the areas that pose the highest risk to your organization. Many hospitals currently do not have such a documentation review in place. If this is the case in your institution, you might want to meet with members of your HIM compliance team to decide which area(s) to pilot for documentation review.

Comparing a patient's documentation to charges billed or recorded for that patient has gained new importance in the past few years. From a compliance perspective, the Office of the Inspector General (OIG) is interested in documentation regardless of the fact that inpatients are reimbursed under the diagnosis-related group (DRG) system, instead of on a charge-by-charge basis. The Health Care Financing Administration (HCFA) uses hospital charges to determine annual changes to both the ICD-9-CM and DRG systems. If facilities do not properly record charges for inpatient stays, changes in the DRG system are not valid.

In addition, one of the most recent compliance initiatives for the government is a concentration on managed care. In particular, the government will compare Medicare managed care cases against DRG-reimbursed patients to determine if there was an under-utilization of services for managed care patients. The government will also perform aggregate analysis of managed care utilization against DRG-reimbursed care. In these analyses, the government will focus on actual charges for inpatient care regardless of whether that care was reimbursed under the DRG system.

As noted above, inpatient records contain documentation from every clinical area in the facility. Some of these clinical areas have a higher compliance risk due to high charges. You might want to include the following high-risk areas in your initial pilot:
- the cardiac catheterization lab;

- supplies (IVs, surgical, large items)—review of nursing documentation;
- interventional radiology; and
- the operating room (OR) and the intensive care unit (ICU).

Once you have decided which area(s) to assess for documentation, you need to coordinate the process with the applicable clinical department. This is the one assessment that the HIM department cannot perform internally. Follow the other steps in the assessment process, as noted on page 69. To get a sense for whether there are inherent risks in the current documentation process, the reviewer needs to perform the assessment concurrently with the clinician documenting the care or treatment. This interviewing stage might be more limited than the interviews you perform in the HIM department. During the documentation assessment you want to identify that

- the physician ordered the care or treatment being delivered;
- the patient received the care or treatment;
- the clinician documented the care or treatment; and
- the clinician performed some transaction that creates a charge for the care or treatment.

Assessment of the completeness of documentation

Another important assessment you must conduct is for the completeness of the medical record. This assessment takes place after the patient has been discharged. Generally, it focuses on these types of documentation issues:

- ensuring the presence of physicians' and other clinicians' signatures;
- ensuring the presence of required reports (e.g., discharge summary, OR reports, the history and physical); and
- getting all necessary test results (e.g., lab, radiology).

Medical records completion is a process that is inherent to the HIM department. The assessment for compliance should carefully track the manual process, making sure to enforce a consistent application of guidelines. For example, if your medical staff bylaws state that physicians will be suspended if they have incomplete records for more than 30 days, is this guideline applied consistently to all physicians? Making exceptions not only places your facility at increased compliance risk, but could also result in added legal liability from the provider.

The final stage in the incomplete documentation assessment is to perform a secondary analysis. After a physician comes in to complete his or her records, your compliance team again reviews each record to verify that the deficiency was completely cured. If so, forward the record to permanent storage. If not, keep the record in the incomplete file area until the physician returns again. Secondary analysis is a process that, if not performed accurately, could place the facility at increased risk. Your team must ensure that staff do not store incomplete records in an area intended for complete file storage.

Your team should perform the analysis for medical record completeness before the coding function. The OIG's *Compliance Program Guidance* states that coding staff should only code *complete patient records*. Every HIM department must reckon with this requirement. It is estimated that approximately 75% of all patient records are coded without (at least) a discharge summary. Pursuant to the *Program Guidance,* the OIG seeks to stop this practice. You must track this information and decide internally how your facility should respond to the OIG's request to not code without complete documentation—including a discharge summary. You will continue to protect your facility from any compliance exposure as long as you are reviewing 100% of the coding.

Assessment of coding and abstracting

The coding and abstracting process, as noted in previous steps in this book, is currently under the highest degree of scrutiny by the OIG. Because the coding process drives reimbursement under the DRG system, the greatest False Claims Act exposure is here.

The first step in the coding assessment process is to assess the current coding staff. It's a good idea to test each coder for basic and advanced coding competencies. Because coders are expected to code any discharge, regardless of specialty, the test should examine a wide range of coding skills. Review the test results with each coder. You must identify any lack of coding competency and act on it immediately. If you identify a coder without the appropriate skill sets to perform a specific job, reassign him or her to a coding duty that has a lower competency level (i.e., from inpatient to clinic visits). Or, you might want to quality-check all of his or her work until that coder has satisfactorily refined his or her skill sets. However, if the coder does not improve after a period of time that your facility determines to be reasonable, you might want to consider terminating that coder.

After the coding competency tests, you must trace the steps of your coders and flow out the process each follows in the coding and abstracting functions. For a sample flowchart of the coding and abstracting process, see Exhibit 4.1. You should watch out for these activities that increase your risk of noncompliance:
- incorrect use of (or lack of use of) resources;
- reliance on a computerized encoder without using a coding book;
- the degree to which staff refer documentation issues and questions to the physicians; and
- review of prior admissions to complete the diagnostic picture.

Exhibit 4.1

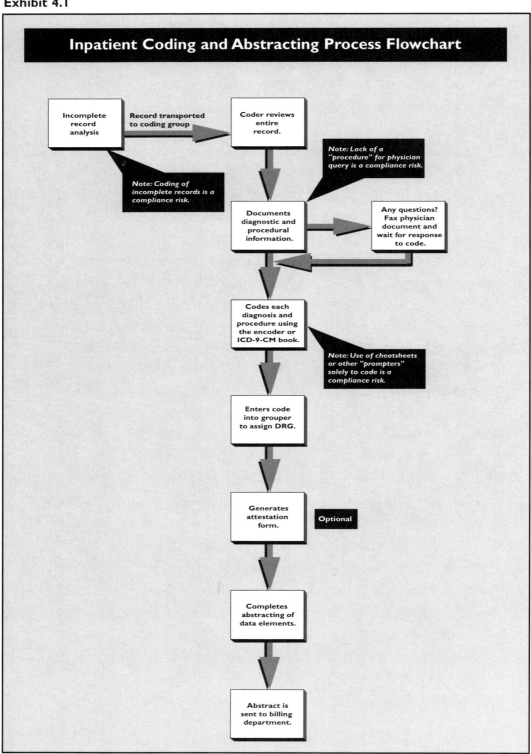

You should assess the abstracting process for any compliance risks as well. In particular, focus on any artificial edits that abstracting staff might use to force the abstracting system to accept codes. Also, if you record ICD-9-CM codes on the patient's record, they should match the codes in the abstracting system exactly.

Focus on key entry methodology for abstracting processes. In particular, is the coder also performing key entry? If yes, you need to pay particular attention to any changes made between the paper copy (if one exists) of the abstract and the computerized entries. Often coders, prompted by computer edits, make changes in the abstracting system. And although these changes might well be correct, the coder should also make the same changes on the paper copy. This preservation of consistency between systems minimizes additional investigation.

Assessment of the release of information

The release of information (ROI) function appears to be a simple process with little or none of the compliance risk that coding has. However, due to the sensitive nature of patient information, this function has the potential to put the facility at an even greater risk of legal liability if not performed properly. Patients own the information in their medical records. Because of this ownership right, they are entitled to protection from that information being released without their consent. Therefore, if this happens and the patient is harmed as a result, the facility could face not only a noncompliance issue with the federal or state governments, but also a civil lawsuit brought by the patient.

Test your staff on their knowledge of ROI laws (both federal and state-specific) to help them understand the importance of this function. Staff who do not pass the minimum competency should have all of their work reviewed until they successfully pass the test. Consider termination as an option for those employees who do not improve.

Track all sources relied upon for ROI authorization. If multiple staff members are responsible for ROI, follow each person's actions to ensure consistency in the process. You might also want to track the use of logs and storage of the release authorization forms. If you outsource your ROI function, be very cautious about firms with high quotas for photocopying. While quotas can ensure a high level of productivity, they can often encourage unacceptable releases of information.

Assessment of record retention and storage

The filing, retrieval, and storage of records is another function that has the potential to place the facility at a high degree of legal liability. Although it might seem to be a simple process, you should test all file staff on their ability to file and retrieve records accurately. Filing a record in the wrong spot could mean a liability issue for the hospital. As noted in **Step 3: Developing Your Standards of Conduct,** the inability to find a patient record will almost always find the court holding in favor of the plaintiff. Most facilities have cured many of these retrieval and retention woes with the use of color coding and terminal digit filing. However, you still need to test your staff on this skill.

You also need to assess your storage mechanism and your process for retrieving an archived record. Your assessment of each of these functions could lead you to the conclusion that your current manual systems might not suit your facility's needs in the future. If so, you might want to consider looking into the options of optical disk imaging or electronic document management.

Include vendors in your assessment

It is important to include any vendor activity in your assessment process. This is particularly true if the vendor plays a regular role in providing services to your department. Assess the vendor against the same criteria as your staff. Remember that you cannot, in most cases, eliminate risk exposure by using a vendor to perform an activity. You should provide feedback to the vendor regarding your findings during the assessment process and hold them to the same remedial work as your staff. If you have retained a firm to provide the assessment process for you, ensure that they do not assess themselves in any area of the department.

For example, in some instances, a vendor might provide an ongoing service in your department, such as for ROI. That same firm might also hold itself out as an operational or compliance assessment expert. If you retain that firm to provide your operational assessment, it's very difficult for the vendor to provide an objective assessment of its own employees' performance. However, some large firms have the ability to "partition off" their audit groups. In this manner, they separate employees who provide ongoing work from those who provide the assessment. In most cases, this is an acceptable approach.

Comparing the assessment to your HIM policies and procedures

Policies and procedures are an important part of the compliance process. In addition to ensuring that your department functions consistently, they serve as part of your compliance documentation. You need to continuously update your policies and procedures to reflect the current status of your department. In particular, compare policies and procedures for these areas of

HIM compliance risk that we addressed in this step to the assessment results:
- content and quality of documentation;
- completeness of documentation;
- coding and abstracting;
- ROI; and
- record retention and storage.

As you complete your assessment process, you need to identify any inconsistencies between the procedures you are assessing and the policy and procedure you have documented for that process. More importantly, if you identify a process that needs modification during the course of your assessment, you must edit the policy and procedure manual accordingly. If you find a practice that has been out of compliance, you should first modify the practice to ensure that it is now in compliance. Then, modify the policy to be consistent with the practice. You must ensure that your policies are always reflective of what you are actually doing.

Assessment review

The assessment process is important not only from a compliance perspective to identify risk, but also from a basic business perspective. You will identify some basic operational concerns during the compliance assessment. You might want to expand the compliance assessment to address all operational issues. The compliance assessment process is further evidence of the fact that "compliance makes good business sense."

Here's a summary of what you've learned in **Step 4:**

- Conduct a compliance assessment for every area of compliance risk in your department.

- Engage an outside firm to provide a validation of the initial assessment process.

- Update your policies and procedures to be reflective of your actual processes.

- Include activities performed by vendors in your department in the assessment process.

— STEP 5 —

Providing Education and Training—The Hub of Compliance

— Step 5 —

Providing Education and Training—
The Hub of Compliance

The Office of the Inspector General's (OIG) *Compliance Program Guidance* states that all healthcare providers should educate their employees on recent developments and appropriate practices in compliance at least once a year. Those employees whose jobs could place the provider at a risk of noncompliance should receive education even more frequently. These employees include
- coders;
- other health information management (HIM) employees;
- patient accounting staff;
- lab registrars;
- finance staff;
- marketing staff;
- human resources staff; and
- contract negotiations staff.

Education programs should be interactive and delivered at the proper level of detail for affected staff. While the facility's compliance officer should organize and coordinate the training sessions, department managers are responsible for knowing what topics their staff need training in and what their strengths are. The sessions should incorporate such teaching tools as tests, real-life examples or case studies, and expert guest speakers to make the sessions more stimulating for participants and to help them learn better.

Managers can use these basic guidelines to develop an ongoing departmental education program:
- start with the basics;
- include current government initiatives;
- include all industry-specific changes in a timely manner;
- review and re-review changes—especially significant ones;

- include a testing or assessment mechanism; and
- design follow-up training based on identified weaknesses.

Education and the HIM department

The OIG has identified several issues that facilities should address in their compliance programs, most of which involve the HIM

Exhibit 5.1

The OIG's List of Compliance Issues

The OIG states that every hospital's compliance program should address the following issues:

- corporate ethics;
- fraud and abuse laws;
- coding and billing processes;
- ethical management styles;
- Medicare reimbursement principles;
- billing Medicare and Medicaid for services not rendered;
- submitting a bill for physician services actually rendered by a nonphysician;
- signing for a physician without physician authorization;
- alterations of medical records;
- providing medications and procedures without proper authorization;
- violating patient transfer policies;
- double billing;
- bundling/unbundling;
- upcoding;
- documentation requirements;
- DRG creep;
- miscoding;
- proper and improper billing for tests and evaluative procedures;
- admission and discharge policies;
- payment policies for physicians;
- medical necessity;
- documentation retention; and
- medical records.

department in some way (see Exhibit 5.1). Most departments in your facility will have their own compliance training sessions. However, because of the HIM department's expertise in some areas (e.g., coding, documentation), you should take responsibility for educating certain other staff groups in addition to your own. You need to focus in particular on groups who affect or are affected by the coding process, such as physicians, ancillary providers, and billing staff.

Physicians

Physicians have always been at the heart of many of the coding problems in HIM departments. Part of the reason for this is that they do not understand the type of documentation that is needed to code appropriately. In the past there was little incentive to entice physicians to cooperate with documentation problems much beyond that of ensuring that they completed their deficiencies. Today, however, physicians have an additional incentive to understand and cooperate with the documentation process; because many are often deficient in documentation, physicians are one of the largest OIG target groups for overbilling.

You need to educate physicians about the importance of complete documentation and Medicare's documentation rules. The federal government expects the documentation included in a patient's medical record to justify the billing. For example, a major piece of information that investigators look for is medical necessity. The physician's documentation must show that services provided were medically necessary.

Before you begin your training sessions, you might want to identify the five or 10 most common physician documentation problems in your facility (see Exhibit 5.2 for some common problems found in many facilities). Do this by speaking to your coding staff or through a coding audit (see **Step 7: Conducting a Compliance Audit).** Once you have done this, you can formulate a plan to eliminate these problems. To help make your plan a success, you might want to enlist the aid of a few influential medical staff leaders. They can guide you in content and be your champion at the presentations. In addition, they can try to enforce, or at least encourage, their physician peers to comply with your documentation standards.

Generally, physician education sessions on documentation work best if you conduct them according to specialty groups or departments. That way, you can use specialty-specific examples, and all physicians in the group can relate to what you are saying. If limited

Exhibit 5.2

Common Documentation Problems for Physicians

The most common documentation problems for physicians in most facilities that result in incorrect coding include the following:

- vague or general diagnoses (when additional descriptors or adjectives would provide more accurate coding);
- a discharge summary containing information about the patient's condition that is not documented in the rest of the record;
- positive test results (e.g., lab, culture and sensitivities) without physician confirmation;
- typed "OR Reports" that contain information additional to what the physician documented in the "op note" (the progress notes) about the procedure;
- inconsistencies between the pathologist's and the attending physician's documentation, or the consultant's and attending physician's documentation;
- documentation of historical diagnoses as though they existed currently; and
- lack of documentation of diagnoses outside the attending specialty (especially true with specialties such as orthopedic surgery, vascular surgery, and neurosurgery).

resources make specialty-specific sessions impossible, you might also consider separating the staff into two main groups—medical physicians and surgical physicians.

Hold your information sessions regularly, remembering to account for the hectic and uncertain schedules of most physicians. Consider using our training suggestions in your sessions. You might also want to serve coffee or snacks to encourage attendance. Consider creating some sort of tool for physicians, such as the "Evaluation and Management Billing Guide" in Exhibit 5.3, that they can easily reference once your sessions are over.

Ancillary providers

All clinicians who treat patients must completely document that treatment in the patient record. Just as physicians do, ancillary providers need education to understand their role in documentation and how it affects the coding process. You can identify the top five or 10 documentation problems for ancillary providers not only through coding audits, but more importantly through reviews for the content and quality of documentation. While you still need physician documentation for many documentation problems, the ancillary provider can often prompt the physician to document as well. Remember, the documentation process should be a team effort!

These are the top two documentation problems for ancillary providers in most facilities:
- nursing documentation of diagnoses that require treatment, assessment, or an increased length of stay *and* affect the diagnosis-related group (DRG) assignment—such as decubitus ulcers; and
- dietary documentation of diagnoses, signs, or symptoms that require treatment, assessment, or an increased length of stay *and* affect DRG assignment—such as malnutrition or vitamin deficiency.

Exhibit 5.3

Evaluation and Management Billing Guide

A. Content key

History (key component—circle one)

Type of history	Key	Definition
(Problem) focused	F	CC, brief history present illness (1–3)
Expanded	E	CC, brief history present illness (1–3); problem-pertinent ROS (1)
Detailed	D	CC, ext. HPI (4+), extended system review (2-9); pertinent past, family, and/or SH (1)
Comprehensive	C	CC, ext. HPI (4+); complete system review (10+); complete past, family, and/or SH (2 or 3)

Examination (key component—circle one)

Type of exam	Key	Definition
(Problem) focused	F	Affected system/body area (1)
Expanded	E	+ Other symptomatic or related system/body area (2-7)
Detailed	D	Extended exam of affected system(s)/body area(s) or related system(s)/body area(s)
Comprehensive	C	Complete single-system specialty exam or complete multisystem exam (>/=8)

Medical decision making (key component—circle one): 2 of 3 required

= Complexity	Key	Diagnosis/options	Data	Risk
Straightforward	S	Minimal($\leq$1)	Minimal/low($\leq$1)	Minimal
Low	L	Limited(2)	Limited(2)	Low
Moderate	M	Multiple(3)	Moderate(3)	Moderate
High	H	Extensive($\geq$4)	Extensive($\geq$4)	High

Reprinted with permission from QuadraMed Corporation. Copyright 1998.

Exhibit 5.3 *continued*

Evaluation and Management Billing Guide

B. Inpatient care

Initial inpatient care: 3 of 3 required

E&M code	History	Exam	Medical decision-making	Average time (in minutes)
99221	D/C	D/C	S or L	30
99222	C	C	M	50
99223	C	C	H	70

Subsequent hospital care: 2 of 3 required

E&M code	History	Exam	Medical decision-making	Average time (in minutes)
99231	F	F	S or L	15
99232	E	E	M	25
99233	D	D	H	35

Initial inpatient consult: 3 of 3 required

E&M code	History	Exam	Medical decision-making	Average time (in minutes)
99251	F	F	S	20
99252	E	E	S	40
99253	D	D	L	55
99254	C	C	M	80
99255	C	C	H	110

Follow-up inpatient consult: 2 of 3 required

E&M code	History	Exam	Medical decision-making	Average time (in minutes)
99261	F	F	S or L	10
99262	E	E	M	20
99263	D	D	H	30

Reprinted with permission from QuadraMed Corporation. Copyright 1998.

Exhibit 5.3 *continued*

Evaluation and Management Billing Guide

C. Outpatient care

Office visit, new patient: 3 of 3 required

E&M code	History	Exam	Medical decision-making	Average time (in minutes)
99201	F	F	S	10
99202	E	E	S	20
99203	D	D	L	30
99204	C	C	M	45
99205	C	C	H	60

Office visit, established patient: 2 of 3 required

E&M code	History	Exam	Medical decision-making	Average time (in minutes)
99211	N/A	N/A	N/A	5
99212	F	F	S	10
99213	E	E	L	15
99214	D	D	M	25
99215	C	C	H	40

Office consult, new or established patient: 3 of 3 required

E&M code	History	Exam	Medical decision-making	Average time (in minutes)
99241	F	F	S	15
99242	E	E	S	30
99243	D	D	L	40
99244	C	C	M	60
99245	C	C	H	80

Emergency department visit: 3 of 3 required (new or established patient)

E&M code	History	Exam	Medical decision-making
99281	F	F	S
99282	E	E	L
99283	E	E	M
99284	C	C	M
99285	C	C	H

Confirmatory consult, any setting new or established patient: 3 of 3 required

E&M code	History	Exam	Medical decision-making
99271	F	F	S
99272	E	E	S
99273	D	D	L
99274	C	C	M
99275	C	C	H

Reprinted with permission from QuadraMed Corporation. Copyright 1998.

Step 5: Providing Education and Training—The Hub of Compliance

Once you identify the documentation goals for ancillary providers, map out a strategy for attacking each problem. While your strategy will vary depending on the department, it might include working with a department manager directly or conducting specialized education sessions for each clinical area.

Billing staff

The type of education that billing staff need depends on their role in the coding process. It is best if billing staff are not involved in the coding process at all—in which case, you have no need to educate them. However, usually due to resource shortages, billing staff are involved—often in one of two ways. For example, billing staff might have to address editing or rejection of claims issues when codes are incorrect or unacceptable. Also, in some patient accounting departments, billing staff are actually responsible for assigning codes to some of the outpatient encounters in a facility. Often, they are assigning ICD-9-CM codes (and sometimes CPT) to ensure that the claims drop for billing purposes.

In the first case, in which billing staff have to address incomplete or incorrect codes via the editing process, they need basic coding education. They need to learn how to use a coding book and how to assign codes correctly, assuming that the original codes (hopefully assigned in the HIM department) were assigned correctly. The billing staff also needs to understand that when they don't have enough information, they should contact the HIM department for assistance.

When patient accounting staff are the ones actually assigning codes, they need to be educated and tested in all basic ICD-9-CM and CPT coding principles. They might also need some additional training in specific subject areas. Training is a rigorous and expensive process. However, allowing uneducated staff to assign codes that determine reimbursement is an enormous risk. Your best bet is to not have the billing staff involved in the coding process at all.

How to accomplish your educational goals—without losing your sanity

The prospect of all this education and training might seem daunting to you at first. You might think, where am I going to find the time, staff, and resources to train the HIM department, never mind educating other staff in the facility? As the HIM director in your organization, it is a good idea to inform all related parties about the role that you and your staff can play in decreasing compliance exposure. You might want to ask them for training suggestions and help in designing educational sessions.

It is particularly important not to get bogged down with political issues. Often, a task can be delayed when it involves interdepartmental communications and cooperation. This is exactly why you must develop and refine communications as a part of your compliance plan. As the HIM director you need to champion all of the compliance causes for which you and your department are the experts—and there are many of them.

Inform management that if you take on this training role and the increased responsibility, you need additional resources. This is a basic business tenet; an increased workload means you need to increase your staff. To receive these additional resources, stress the importance of the compliance function and remind management that it's better to spend a small amount on training now, rather than millions in fines and loss of reputation later. The OIG's *Compliance Program Guidance* states that every facility is expected to implement an effective compliance plan—

Step 5: Providing Education and Training—The Hub of Compliance

regardless of the cost to the facility. It basically states, "We know compliance can be expensive, but we think it's worth the additional expenditures."

If you are unable to garner the time and staff to conduct the educational sessions and other related tasks described above, your facility could contract out the education function. If you do, remember to completely assess any firm that provides compliance education for your organization. You need to validate a firm's credentials, experience, and reputation. This is an area of significant risk for your organization; you could increase that risk by contracting with an unqualified vendor.

Tracking compliance education

It is essential that you document all compliance activities. If your facility is ever investigated, this documentation proves your commitment to compliance. When tracking compliance education, include certain elements substantiating that you have met all requirements for compliance topics and attendance. For a sample compliance education session track sheet, see Exhibit 5.4.

You should document all of this information and preserve it for at least the statute of limitations for the False Claims Act (up to 10 years). While you could keep the information on paper, an electronic format helps you to store and to preserve it longer and more efficiently. You need to keep evidence of all HIM-specific sessions, as well as any sessions that the HIM staff conducts for other departments. You also need to pass this information on to the corporate compliance officer. As a result, a networked system is the most effective method for storing and communicating education information.

Exhibit 5.4

Compliance Education Session Track Sheet

Topic: _____
Date: _____
Length: _____

Instructor: _____
Group: _____

Goals and objectives
_____
_____
_____
_____

Agenda
_____
_____
_____
_____
_____
_____

Names of attendees
1. _____
2. _____
3. _____
4. _____
5. _____
6. _____
7. _____
8. _____
9. _____
10. _____

Step 5: Providing Education and Training—The Hub of Compliance

HIM credentialing, continuing education, and training responsibilities

In the HIM department there are many functions that require initial and continuous training (see **Steps 3** and **4**). These are the general areas within the HIM department that need their own focus for education:
- content and quality of documentation;
- completeness of documentation;
- coding and abstracting;
- release of information (ROI); and
- record retention and storage.

In addition to tracking continuous training of the staff in each functional area of the HIM department, you also need to track continuing education for credentialed staff. Credentialed staff include those who are credentialed by both the American Health Information Management Association (AHIMA) and the American Academy of Professional Coders (AAPC). AHIMA credentials include registered record administrator (RRA), accredited record technician (ART), certified coding specialist (CCS), and certified coding specialist—physician-based (CCS-P). AAPC credentials include certified professional coder (CPC) and certified professional coder-hospital (CPC-H). Depending on the credential, staff are required to complete between 10 to 40 hours of continuing education credits per year.

Credentialing staff in the coding function is of critical concern. The OIG's *Compliance Program Guidance* states that only appropriately credentialed and trained staff should perform the coding function. Many HIM departments require their coding staff to obtain one of the coding credentials in addition to the HIM credential. The primary coding credentials are CCS for hospital coding, CPC or CCS-P for physician coding, and CPC-H for hospital CPT coding. As the number of credentials increases for your staff, the number of credit hours to maintain these credentials increases. You need to create a plan that not only meets the needs of your staff, but is also efficient and cost-beneficial for your organization.

You need to design a plan for credentialing, continuing education, and training in your department. Use the information gathered during your compliance assessments to determine your staff's baseline training needs. Use the credentialing requirements to determine baseline continuing education needs. Work these requirements into each employee's annual goals and objectives. Then, design a system of checks to ensure that employees attend relevant and required continuing education and training sessions. Document these sessions and make them a permanent piece of your compliance program files. For a sample employee attendance track sheet that you could adapt for your department, see Exhibit 5.5.

Educational resources to help you perform the job correctly

Resources play a significant role in the educational requirements for compliance programs; to perform a job correctly, employees need to have access to the appropriate resources. This is particularly true in the HIM department. The federal government and the American Medical Association (AMA) make changes to the ICD-9-CM and CPT coding systems at least once a year. And, interpretations of changes, guidelines, and other relevant information from the *Federal Register* are published throughout the year. You can provide this information to staff in the form of books, periodicals, and other documents, as well as through computer programs and Internet access. See Exhibit 5.6 for a list of coding compliance resources.

These resources, coupled with the compliance assessment, continuing education, and training programs, help to ensure that

Exhibit 5.5

Employee Attendance Track Sheet

Place a ✔ under those training sessions that each employee attended.

Employee and Title	Training session name and date	
	Coding Compliance Training Session, 2/26/98	CCS Continuing Education Seminar, 4/8/98
Sample: Joe Smith, Inpatient Coder	✔	✔

Exhibit 5.6

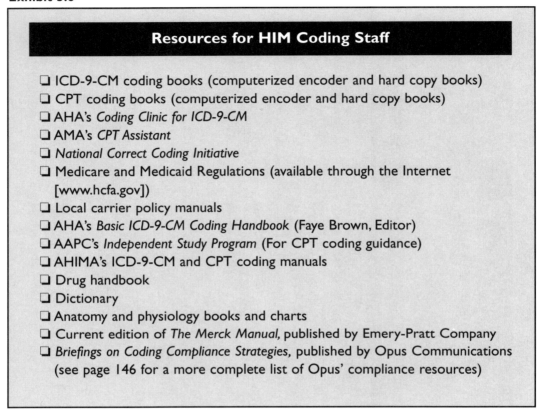

your staff have the ability to perform their jobs correctly. Once your staff have the ability and the resources, you will learn how to ensure that they perform their jobs correctly on a continuous basis (see **Step 6**).

Education and training review

In **Step 5** you learned the following:

- Education plays a central role in ensuring the success of your compliance program.

- Staff need ongoing education in all functional areas of your HIM department.

Step 5: Providing Education and Training—The Hub of Compliance

- The HIM department needs to play a key role in developing educational programs for staff throughout your facility, including
    - physicians;
    - ancillary providers;
    - nursing staff; and
    - billing staff.

- You need to track all HIM educational compliance activities.

- Comprehensive and up-to-date resources are an essential element of compliance education.

— STEP 6 —

Ongoing Monitoring—Keeping Your House in Order

— STEP 6 —

Ongoing Monitoring—Keeping Your House in Order

Ongoing monitoring is an intrinsic part of your compliance process. If designed correctly, your monitoring plan can ensure that you remain compliant in any risk-bearing procedures. Initially, you need to differentiate the ongoing monitoring process from the auditing process, which we describe in more detail in **Step 7.**

Auditing is an infrequent, retrospective review usually conducted by an outside firm; ongoing monitoring is a regular, internal review of data to ensure correctness and completeness. Because the goal of a monitoring program is to prevent noncompliant data from being submitted for payment, you need to perform the correctness and completeness reviews concurrently. Compliance monitoring is a cost-beneficial process for your department that will help ensure
- ongoing data quality;
- clear performance expectations of and from your staff;
- a pipeline of information for compliance education; and
- enhanced departmental communication.

Where do I begin?

It is common to feel overwhelmed at the thought of creating yet another process within the usually overburdened health information management (HIM) department. However, because of the nature of the HIM department and its functions, most HIM professionals are very good at developing monitoring processes. In fact, your department probably has many of the needed processes in place already; you might just need to enhance the documentation and feedback portions. Follow the tips in Exhibit 6.1 to help you to take stock of your current monitoring procedures.

Exhibit 6.1

Analysis of Your Current Monitoring Process

1. List all monitoring processes currently in place in your department;

2. Analyze the contents of those processes;

3. Determine the parts of the processes that you should retain;

4. Assess where there are "holes"—areas that need to be enhanced in the monitoring process; and

5. Decide if any of the current processes can be eliminated and where new processes are needed.

Analyzing your current monitoring processes is a good exercise for your HIM compliance team. It will help them to develop and maintain a strong overall commitment to compliance. However, your HIM supervisors might need some additional guidance in redesigning the monitoring process as well. You might consider giving them some general guidelines to remember, such as those in Exhibit 6.2.

The remainder of **Step 6** addresses each area in the HIM department that you need to monitor:
- content and quality of documentation;
- completeness of documentation;
- coding and abstracting;
- release of information (ROI); and
- record retention and storage.

The sections are written with respect to current and potential areas of exposure. Note that at any time the government could add additional risk areas to its target investigations. You must keep abreast of these by following the Office of the Inspector General's (OIG)

Step 6: Ongoing Monitoring—Keeping Your House in Order

Compliance Program Guidance, as well as by keeping track of new investigations by the U.S. Attorney's Office.

These are the topics that we will address for each focus area:
- What should be monitored?
- Who should perform the monitoring?
- When and how often should the monitoring take place?
- What format should the monitoring take?

Exhibit 6.2

Four General Guidelines for HIM Supervisors

1. Establish your baseline criteria

All monitoring needs to start with a valid established baseline. Here are some examples:
- monthly case mix of 1.5;
- coding proficiency of 95% for each coder;
- retrieval rate of 100% from permanent files; and
- "x" number of ROI requests processed per day per ROI clerk.

2. Investigate any deviations

You need to examine any deviations from the baseline (up or down) to determine if there is either a problem with performance or a need to redefine the baseline.

3. Determine areas of weakness

Use the results of your initial assessments to determine areas of weakness, then focus your efforts on these areas first until you see an improvement in results.

4. Search for clues to any additional problems

Design your reviews to allow the reviewer to continue to search for possible clues to additional problems. For example, although you might use a focused sampling process, you must always include some degree of random sampling as well.

Once you complete the monitoring process for each of the five HIM risk areas, you must educate staff on the results of the monitoring. You also need to record and preserve your monitoring information, as well as any follow-up education. These processes will be addressed after the above topics.

Monitoring for the content and quality of documentation

Your HIM department should monitor the content and quality of documentation in your facility; you're probably doing it already. However, if you have insufficient resources to undertake the entire process now, first determine which documentation processes carry the highest degree of risk. Then, approach your superior or the facility's compliance committee with a plan to curtail that risk and a request for additional staff in your department to effectively and efficiently undertake that monitoring process.

What should be monitored?

Organizations have different documentation review needs because of managed care and other third-party payer agreements. Also, certain states have additional documentation review needs based upon reimbursement by charges. The fact that Medicare inpatient care is reimbursed based on the diagnosis-related group (DRG) system is not a reason to skip the review of Medicare inpatient documentation. The OIG's *Compliance Program Guidance* addresses the importance of accurate documentation of care reflected in inpatient "charges." The reason for this is that annual updating and calculation of norms for the Prospective Payment System are driven by actual charges. As with compliance, tracking actual charges makes good business sense; it helps the organization measure its efficiency in resource utilization.

Step 6: Ongoing Monitoring—Keeping Your House in Order

For compliance purposes, you should review any documentation that is the basis for the generation of a bill for patient care. This type of review is different from the type of review that occurs for coding purposes. Your documentation monitoring, performed concurrently, should be poised to ensure that the full extent of the care provided is reflected in the documentation. You also need to ensure the reverse—that the documentation does not overstate the care provided. And, of course, you can review additional documentation for quality of care purposes. At a minimum, you should monitor the following types of documentation concurrently:

- documentation generating inpatient charges (especially bigger ticket items);
- documentation for any physician charges (if the organization employs physicians and bills for their services); and
- documentation for ancillary service billings.

Who should conduct the monitoring?

The HIM department should manage documentation monitoring. However, it is important to involve expert clinical staff when necessary. This not only validates your process, but also involves more of your organization's staff in the compliance process. You might only need to involve clinical staff for certain pieces of the review or to participate in the quality assurance (QA) process. For example, you might need to involve certain clinicians, such as registered nursing staff, physical therapists, and other ancillary service staff, to review some specialized clinical documentation.

When and how often should the monitoring take place?

Documentation monitoring should occur in a three-step process:
1. The reviewer monitors the care process.
2. The clinician documents the care.

109

3. The reviewer compares all documentation with his or her observation of the care process.

If possible, the reviewer should share the results of the review with the clinician immediately. However, because most patient care situations do not allow for this type of intervention, reviewers often compile their results to share with clinicians retrospectively.

The monitoring process should occur at the same time that the clinician provides the care. The results of the initial monitoring process will determine the frequency of the ongoing process. If the results are good, documentation does not have to be monitored as frequently for content and quality. Less favorable results, however, will require more frequent monitoring and remedial action.

The frequency of documentation is also driven by the availability of resources. This monitoring process tends to be the most resource-consumptive because of the concurrent and interactive nature of the process. As a result, budgetary constraints might only allow for an initial "pilot" monitoring. In other instances, facilities might elect to provide documentation monitoring once or twice a year for each nursing floor or medical specialty. Remember, it is more important to get the process started than to agonize over the frequency of the reviews. Once you have some baseline information, you can roll out additional reviews.

What format should the monitoring take?

Ideally, the HIM staff should have access to records on the patient care unit and be able to interact with physicians and other clinicians at the time of document entry. There are appropriate times for the monitoring process to take place that will make the process and staff interaction more effective—such as during grand round sessions. Grand rounds are held regularly—either every week or every month, depending on the specialty. Try to schedule 10 to 15 minutes

Step 6: Ongoing Monitoring—Keeping Your House in Order

of each session to address specific patient documentation issues with physicians either individually or in groups. You could have the same kind of documentation session with clinical groups (e.g., nursing).

You need to find a scheduled time that fits into the mainstream of activities on the floor, bearing in mind that you must adjust to the clinicians' schedules. You need to understand the schedule of events and find the right clinical person (e.g., a nurse manager) to tell you the approach that will work best on a particular unit. Organizing the monitoring process will take time initially, but once you do, it will fit right into the clinicians' activity schedule and become as much a part of their routine as seeing patients—as it should.

You need to monitor and record individual episodes of care separately. It's important to categorize certain data elements for aggregate reporting. For example, for each episode monitored, you should record such quantifiable data elements as the type of deficiency, the reason for the deficiency, and the consequences of the deficiency. This last one is especially important; if the deficiency is not corrected, it could induce a monetary payment. Having these elements documented helps you to educate staff and follow up on problems and improvements. It could also help you to determine focused samples for the future. See Exhibit 6.3 for a sample form.

For this type of review, you also want to include a narrative explanation of suggested changes. You might want to include a copy of the documentation before and after the monitoring process.

Exhibit 6.3

Documentation Content and Quality Deficiency Form

Medical record number: _____ Date: _____

Name of physician/clinician: _____

Name of reviewer: _____

Type of deficiency: _____

Reason for the deficiency

_____
_____
_____
_____

Consequences of the deficiency

_____
_____
_____
_____

Recommended correction

_____
_____
_____
_____

Monitoring for the completeness of documentation

What should be monitored?

Standard medical record deficiency reviews are probably sufficient for monitoring the completeness of documentation. Your

Step 6: Ongoing Monitoring—Keeping Your House in Order

department should be conducting a daily deficiency and analysis review on the record of every discharged patient. Generally, the standards for this review are determined by some combination of the following:
- Medicare Conditions of Participation;
- state licensure regulations;
- Joint Commission on Accreditation of Healthcare Organizations (JCAHO) standards; and
- the medical staff bylaws.

From a compliance perspective, the government's focus is on incomplete documentation that could void a charge for patient care. This documentation primarily includes signatures on orders as well as valid orders for all patient treatment. As a result you might want to increase your focus on these kinds of documentation. In addition, your monitoring should extend to all patient encounters—including outpatient visits—and not just focus on inpatient stays.

Who should conduct the monitoring?
A supervisor in the HIM department is probably the most effective person to monitor for record completeness. Because this function is usually performed regularly in the department, many staff are familiar with it. If you have a small department without the appropriate supervisor, you could train a staff member to regularly monitor a random sampling of all records.

When and how often should the monitoring take place?
You should regularly monitor documentation for completeness, pursuant to the OIG's *Compliance Program Guidance*. For the average HIM department, this could mean anything from weekly to monthly, depending on the sample size. If you are counting each record as "one" in your population, you probably need to review about 10% to 30% of discharges. Every record is reviewed by a records completion clerk for completion, but this is a review of first impression.

Monitoring by its very nature is a review of second impression. You don't need to (and probably don't want to) monitor 100%—that would mean that every record was looked at twice for completion.

You might want to start out with 30% and work toward 10%. Simple random sample selections refer to 20% as a representative sample. In this case, each deficiency counts as one, so by reviewing "records" instead of deficiencies, you still have a representative random sample selection. Also, remember to consider what degree of risk the particular activity contains when determining sample size.

You have sufficient data in the department to calculate a valid baseline for expected deficiencies. If you have deviations from your baseline, you need to monitor a larger sample more frequently until you determine the reason for that deviation.

What format should the monitoring take?

Monitoring can be as simple as an additional review of all of the deficiencies that the analyst originally flagged. You need to record any deviations on an audit form, categorizing errors and changes by type. Here are some examples of types of changes for the completeness of documentation:
- request for progress note signatures missed;
- request for operative report missed;
- request for co-signatures missed; and
- request for nursing note signature missed.

Weigh each type of error to arrive at a consistent rating system. For example, you might rate a request for a discharge summary or operative report as more serious than a missing request for a nursing note signature. An audit form can assist you in tracking any existing trends. While you can perform the entire process manually, you will have a more complete and reliable system if you record the results in a database or spreadsheet. See Exhibit 6.4 for a sample form.

Exhibit 6.4

Compliance Documentation Completeness Review Form

Reviewed by: _____ Date: _____

Signature: _____

Medical record #	D/C date	Cons	Ancil	DS	H&P	OR	PN	Other	DS	OR	H&P	Cons	Ancill	Other	>2 days without PN	Comments	Total
Total																	

Types of deficiencies reported missing

Reprinted with permission from QuadraMed Corporation. Copyright 1997.

Monitoring coding and abstracting

What should be monitored?

You probably already conduct some regular monitoring of your coding activity. Check the current process to ensure that it meets the requirements for your compliance program. You also need to keep abreast of OIG work plans and current investigations and modify your coding monitoring process accordingly.

Case mix tracking

Your monitoring process should start with a validated case mix index (CMI) for inpatient cases. The case mix benchmark should include these criteria:
- the average relative weight (the most common calculation of case mix);
- percentage of discharges by specialty (will allow you to track potential causes for changes to the CMI);
- average length of stay; and
- average charges.

In addition to the ongoing monitoring of coding processes, you need to establish valid baseline averages for the CMI data. Then, you can track any deviations from these aggregate numbers. Based on deviations, you might need to increase your sample selection as well as the frequency of your reviews until you have either identified the cause for deviation or determined a new validated baseline. Remember, several factors other than coding can affect CMI baselines, such as
- changes in admitting patterns by physicians of a certain specialty (e.g., groups leave, join, etc.);
- new services that the facility offers; and
- general changes in admission patterns overall (e.g., seasonal changes).

Coding monitoring

In addition to the case mix tracking, you also need to conduct a concurrent review of coding activities for all types of patient encounters. You should regularly review these types of cases:

For inpatient cases, review all ICD-9-CM coding for both the patient's diagnoses and procedures that were originally coded.

Inpatient cases (reimbursed by the DRG system):
- principal diagnosis of 482.89 (other specified bacterial pneumonia) and 482.83 (gram negative pneumonia);
- principal diagnosis of 038.9 (unspecified sepsis) with a secondary diagnosis of 599.0 (urinary tract infection);
- A randomized sampling of cases (whenever you identify a pattern in the errors, add those types of cases to each monitoring session); and
- a sampling of cases with the following criteria:
    - DRG 475 (respiratory diagnosis with ventilator) with a secondary diagnosis of 428.0 (congestive heart failure); and
    - DRG 87 (respiratory failure) with a secondary diagnosis of 496 (chronic obstructive pulmonary disease [COPD]) or 428.0 (congestive heart failure).

For outpatient cases, review both ICD-9-CM diagnostic coding and CPT procedural coding for all outpatient services rendered. The emphasis for outpatient reviews is on the CPT coding because these codes determine reimbursement.

Outpatient cases:
- unbundled CPT codes;
- CPT codes not meeting medical necessity criteria;
- cases without diagnostic-procedure linkage; and
- ambulatory surgery center (ASC), ambulatory patient group (APG), or ambulatory patient classification (APC) outliers.

Who should conduct the monitoring?

Generally, the coding supervisor is the best individual to conduct ongoing coding monitoring, as he or she is usually responsible for conducting some sort of review or monitoring process. Even if your department's coding supervisor is not responsible for the compliance monitoring process, it should fit easily into his or her current responsibilities. Your coding supervisor most likely already has experience with the review process and with providing feedback to the reviews. This familiarity will make your compliance monitoring more effective and efficient.

When and how often should the monitoring take place?

There are two interests in the coding compliance area: the financial needs of the organization to generate bills efficiently and the desire of the HIM professional to ensure data quality in all coding functions. Often, these interests are at odds. To decide how often you should monitor your coding process, you need to consider these factors:

- the number of coders you have;
- the complexity of the patient cases;
- the results of your initial compliance assessment; and
- the number of different locations and departments in which coding is performed at your facility.

Tailor the frequency of your reviews according to your department's needs. There is value to performing some degree of daily monitoring. Given your staffing situation and responses to the issues above, you might be able to perform very focused reviews daily and add random larger samples monthly.

What format should the monitoring take?

Before you embark on your coding monitoring process, you must first decide on your goals, aside from the obvious goal of ensuring

Step 6: Ongoing Monitoring—Keeping Your House in Order

compliant coding. You can ensure compliance by identifying potentially noncompliant coding and then educating staff about those findings. You can continue reviews to ensure not only that the same errors do not occur, but also that you identify any new issues and deal with them in a timely manner.

Here are some other goals you might have for your coding monitoring program:
- trending your results by coder;
- trending your results by physician;
- tracking documentation issues by specific document;
- determining the reasons for coding changes (e.g., the coding guideline was not applied appropriately or there was no documentation to support the assigned code); and
- determining the type of coding change (e.g., principal diagnosis, addition or deletion of a complication or comorbidity).

The goals you set for your monitoring process determine the extent of your program. The more data you collect, the more inferences and business decisions you can make. There is significant value to consistently collecting data elements for compliance, department management, and decision-making in every area of the organization that affects patient care. At a minimum you will need to
- design an audit form or database screen to use to collect the data for each record reviewed (see Exhibit 6.5);
- document the procedures for using that form and for the collection of all data elements to ensure consistent use of the form;
- review records that were pulled according to your pre-established sample selection methodology;
- record the results of the review;
- calculate the results of the review;
- analyze the results, make recommendations, and decide on appropriate follow-up plans;
- disseminate the results to relevant parties;

Exhibit 6.5

DRG/Data Quality Audit Worksheet

Facility: Sample hospital

Name: Sample, Name	Admit date: 02/24/1998
Bill#: 10085703406	Discharge date: 03/06/1998
MR#: 00035062241	Disposition: 1
Payor: MD97	Birth date: 11/10/1935
Phys: Welby	Age in years: 62
Coder: HC	Length of stay: 10
Auditor: JD	Total charge: 9,409

Orginal DRG:	463 - Signs & symptoms W CC
Estimated DRG:	182 - Esophagitis, gastroent & misc digest disorders Age>17 W CC.
Reason for review:	What was the cause of the symptom? See Coding Clinic 1st Qtr, 1991.
Look for codes:	5589 P - Noninf gastroenterit nec 53010 P - Esophagitis, unspecified
	5641 P - Irritable colon 792 P - ABN find-stool contents

	Original diags	Audit diags	Doc type/date	I.	II.	III.	IV.
1	7895						
	Ascites						
2	4254 CC						
	Prim cardiomyopathy nec						
3	585 CC						
	Chronic renal failure						
4	4280 CC						
	Congestive heart failure						
5	496 CC						
	Chr airway obstruct nec						
6	5997 CC						
	Hematuria						
7							
8							
9							
10							

	Original procs	Audit procs	Doc type/date	I.	II.	III.	IV.
1	5491						
	Percu abdominal drainage						
2							
3							
4							
5							
6							
7							
8							
9							
10							

Exhibit 6.5 *continued*

DRG/Data Quality Audit Worksheet

I. Type of change

- A: Add
- C: Combo codes
- D: Delete
- O: Other change
- P: Principal DX
- W: Change code then declare it as PDX
- N: Add combo code
- Q: Add Principal DX
- S: Combo with PDX
- V: Change then combine
- Change/combo/PDX

If (A) then you must complete section II.

II. Secondary DX

- A: Clinical evaluation
- B: Therapeutic treatment
- C: Diagnostic procedures
- D: Extended LOS
- E: Increased care/monitoring
- F: Other coding guidelines

*Based on UHDDS guidelines

III. Reason for coding change

- A: Documentation available at time of coding
- B: MD verification needed
- C: No documentation to support coding
- D: Clerical error
- E: Documentation interpretation
- F: Documentation not available at time of coding

If (A) or (E) complete Coding Guidelines
If (B) complete the Physician Guidelines

IV: Documentation issues

- A: More specific DX or PX
- B: PDX definition not applied correctly

Coding Guidelines
- C: Coexisting PDXs
- D: 4th or 5th digit error
- E: Other coding conv. not applied correctly
- F: Documented procedure performed

Physician Guidelines
- G: +Lab report, but no MD verification
- H: +C&S, but not MD verification
- I: +Radiology rpt, but not MD verification
- J: +Cardiology rpt, but not MD verification
- K: +Other ancil rpt, but not MD verification
- L: +Nurses note, but no MD verification
- M: +Consult—no attending confirmation
- N: Other documentation issues

V. DRG calculations

	Orginal	Estimated	Revised
DRG	463	182	
Weight	0.6907	0.7664	

If there is a DRG change then you must complete Section VI.

VI. General reason for DRG change

- ___ PDX change
- ___ Add CC
- ___ Delete CC
- ___ Secondary DX change
- ___ Discharge status
- ___ Add OR
- ___ Delete OR
- ___ Change OR
- ___ Key entry

Comments

Document types: PN, H&P, Consult, ER, Lab/Med, Anes, NN, Order, C&S, Facesheet, Path, OR, DS, Rad, Card, other
☐ Check if MD review is required ☐ Check if DQ review
Name: _____ Title: _____ Date: _____

This is a recommended coding/DRG change only. The hospital shall make the final and ultimate decision as to whether to accept our recommendation(s). The hospital assumes all liability and is solely responsible for resubmitting/rebilling any recommended changes.

Reprinted with permission from QuadraMed Corporation. Copyright 1998.

- proceed with follow-up plans; and
- proceed with the next review according to the same criteria listed above.

Monitoring the release of information process

What should be monitored?

The biggest compliance and legal risk for ROI is releasing confidential patient information without the appropriate consent of the patient or legal representative. Therefore, the monitoring process should focus on a comparison of the released documents with the consent forms on file.

Who should conduct the monitoring?

The HIM supervisor for the ROI function, or another department member who is knowledgeable about the laws and guidelines governing ROI can effectively conduct the monitoring process.

When and how often should the monitoring take place?

The baseline for ROI is that 100% of the documents released will have the necessary consents in the appropriate format, as required by law, accrediting bodies, and internal policy. Any deviation from this standard is a compliance disaster.

The results of your initial monitoring reviews and compliance assessments will determine how frequently you need to monitor the ROI function. ROI monitoring should be conducted before records are released. Review a sample at least quarterly. However, if you identify any deviations, you might need to monitor weekly or even more frequently, until you identify a definite increase in compliance processing.

What format should the monitoring take?

Develop an audit form that will help you to collect necessary data elements (see Exhibit 6.6). You also need to conduct a review on the records that have been processed but not yet mailed. To ensure that your results are not skewed, staff cannot know that the review occurs on the day they are performing the actual work.

You might also want to review "rejected" ROI requests. Any time a request is made and rejected, document the reason for rejection in the ROI database. This information, as well as information for released records, should be consistent with laws and regulations.

Monitoring the record retention and storage process

What should be monitored?
The ability to locate a patient record is important not only from a compliance perspective, but from a purely legal perspective as well. Retention and storage monitoring should focus on
- the ability to retrieve all types of records from permanent and incomplete storage; and
- the completeness of records in incomplete storage (especially records that have been microfilmed or imaged).

Who should conduct the monitoring?
The supervisor of the record retention and storage function in the HIM department could effectively perform this review, but you might also want to train additional staff as well. By distributing the responsibility for retention and storage to several people, you send the message throughout the department of how significant is the ability to retrieve patient records.

When and how often should the monitoring be performed?
The baseline for retrieving patient records is 100%. While you should review a sampling of records at least quarterly, you might need to conduct monthly reviews if you identify an error rate

Exhibit 6.6

HIM Compliance Release of Information Review Form

Reviewed by: _____ Date: _____

Medical record #	Discharge date	No author	Authorized but wrong signature	No re-release statement on authorization	Other author problem	HIV req. not met	Psych. req. not met	Etoh/drug req. not met	Entire record referenced only a portion requested	Comments	Totals
Total											

Reprinted with permission from QuadraMed Corporation. Copyright 1998.

Step 6: Ongoing Monitoring—Keeping Your House in Order

greater than 2% (or whatever level you set as your acceptable baseline rate). Any deviation from this baseline is a compliance crisis and could be a major legal crisis as well. The results of your initial monitoring and compliance assessment determine the frequency of your ongoing monitoring process.

Chances are that during your reviews, you will identify situations that might increase the risk of not finding a record. For example, you located the record, but it was in the research room, although your system recorded it as being in permanent files. It is just as important that you act and educate staff on these situations as it is in the cases when you cannot locate a record at all.

What format should the monitoring take?

Select a random sampling of each type of patient record from the master patient index for retrieval. Then, either retrieve the record yourself or have a staff member do so. Whoever is responsible for retrieval should record similar data elements for each case retrieved. For a sample audit/review form, see Exhibit 6.7. Here are some easy-to-collect elements that you might want to record:
- the length of time for retrieval (you probably already collect this information);
- the location of the record (was the record where it should have been? If not, where was it?); and
- unusual circumstances surrounding the retrieval.

You might also want to include a review of the record sign-out process. While some of this should have been addressed during your assessment phase, reviewing a few entries per month to validate the process will refine your monitoring process.

Exhibit 6.7

Compliance Record Retention Audit/Review Form

Reviewed by: _____ **Date:** _____

	Medical record #	D/C date	Record located	Record not located	Comments	Totals
1						
2						
3						
4						
5						
6						
7						
8						
9						
10						
11						
12						
13						
14						
15						
16						
17						
18						
19						
20						
21						
22						
23						
24						
25						
Total						

Reprinted with permission from QuadraMed Corporation. Copyright 1998.

Educating relevant staff on the results of the monitoring

It's important to educate relevant HIM staff on any changes or errors found in the different focus areas during the monitoring process. You must keep track of the types of changes employees make so that in follow-up monitoring you can determine if they made any improvements. If not, you need to take the appropriate disciplinary action.

Timely education of staff on the results of the monitoring process is extremely important. For example, you need to educate coding staff one-on-one regarding their coding changes, and on the results of the monitoring process regularly (weekly at first, then monthly). These educational sessions are the perfect time to include *Coding Clinic* updates and recent Health Care Financing Administration (HCFA) directives. You also need to educate everyone who documents in the patient record, such as physicians, nursing staff, ancillary therapists, other clinicians, and ward clerks. You can combine the results from monitoring for coding and for documentation in most of these educational sessions.

You might also want to use the monitoring process to educate other departments, such as billing staff. As the HIM director, it's your responsibility to deter risk-bearing activity in areas under your control throughout the organization. Given the difficulty of getting different departments (and staff within those departments) together for training sessions, you need to be creative and flexible in your approach.

For example, you might need to hold early morning and late night sessions to accommodate the schedules of clinicians. You could also create some tools that staff members can keep in their pockets or at their stations for easy reference to the monitoring concerns (such as Exhibit 5.3, page 90). Pocket tools can not only ensure that staff remember the significance of the monitoring review, but also that the focus areas are compliant. In addition, you could develop a brief newsletter, memo, or e-mail message containing monitoring results to send to staff in different departments. These tools could supplement or even replace your review sessions, depending on your resources.

Recording and preserving monitoring information

Pursuant to the *Compliance Program Guidance,* you must preserve all monitoring information. From the OIG's perspective, this is the evidence that you have conducted the monitoring as part of your compliance plan. From your perspective, it makes good business sense to record and preserve this information. You need to save this documentation for at least 10 years—the statute of limitations for the False Claims Act.

At a minimum, you must preserve these data elements for all compliance education sessions as evidence that you have followed up on any identified deficiencies. Preserving such information will help to curtail a reoccurrence in the future. To keep track of this data, you might consider using a form similar to that in Exhibit 5.4, "Compliance Education Session Track Sheet" (page 96).

You should preserve all of the information that you collect during the monitoring process, as well as all follow-up education. You should be able to actually reconstruct your entire monitoring process, if necessary, with your preserved documentation. The best way to store your information is electronically. A combination of word processing and database storage with imaging of actual documentation is probably the safest way to ensure your information will be duly preserved.

Step 6: Ongoing Monitoring—Keeping Your House in Order

Ongoing monitoring review

In **Step 6,** you learned the basics of developing an HIM compliance monitoring process:

- Select the right individuals to conduct monitoring in your HIM department.

- Develop baseline rates for each HIM functional area.

- Identify the specific processes that you should monitor.

- Determine the frequency of reviews.

- Select valid and reliable samples.

- Educate staff on monitoring results.

- Record and preserve monitoring information, as well as follow-up education.

— STEP 7 —

Conducting a Compliance Audit

— Step 7 —

Conducting a Compliance Audit

Compliance auditing is the formalized review of data and other functions that have the potential to place the organization at a risk of noncompliance. Generally, auditing occurs at regular intervals to allow for comparison among different time frames. Common audit time frames are quarterly, semi-annually, and annually.

The auditing process differs from ongoing monitoring in several ways. Auditing is a more structured, formal reporting process that
- is usually performed retrospectively;
- is usually conducted by an external entity to ensure objectivity;
- is focused on larger populations and therefore, usually has a larger sample selection; and
- is performed less frequently than monitoring.

A word of caution

You should not undertake the auditing process unless your organization is ready to fully embrace compliance. By law, you must act on the results of any audits within 60 days of the date on which you became aware of improper billing, coding, or other related activities. This includes the willingness to repay any monies that you might have collected in error. This type of repayment is an expected part of the ongoing process; the government traditionally does not view a repayment during an established compliance program as singling out your facility as a target for investigation.

The attorney-client privilege

Some facilities retain external firms through their outside counsel to perform their audits. In this arrangement, the work of the audit firm is considered part of the attorney's work product, which is protected under the attorney-client privilege and is considered to be nondiscoverable. While there are advantages to this type of protection, there are many problems with the attorney-client privilege that should cause you to think carefully before deciding to embark on such an arrangement. For example:

- If your organization disseminates the audit information beyond the highest level of administration in the organization, the attorney-client privilege is destroyed.

- The privilege has not protected information from being discovered or revealed in environmental industry compliance issues.

- You must abandon the attorney-client privilege if the government is to enter into settlement negotiations with your organization.

Do we need an outside audit firm?

You can compare compliance audits to the financial audits that your organization undergoes each year. In the case of financial audits, your organization retains financial experts to perform the audit and to ensure that the written financial statement is an accurate reflection of your organization's financial state during the time period in question (generally a year). A savvy organization views the compliance audit in much the same way. It retains a firm with noted expertise in compliance auditing to record results for any third parties to review, if such information is requested. The question that your organization needs to address—knowing the significance of the compliance process—is, "Can we afford *not* to retain an outside firm to perform compliance audits?"

Once your organization has decided to retain outside experts to perform the compliance audit, you must create the criteria for

selection. Your organization's entire compliance committee should be involved in determining the criteria as well as in selecting the firm. While it is more efficient and effective for your organization to retain one firm for all of its compliance auditing, given the specific nature of many of the functions included in the HIM compliance audit, it is often necessary to retain more than one firm to provide that auditing. The initial year of HIM compliance auditing for an acute-care facility should include auditing and reporting of
- all billing functions;
- all coding functions;
- content and quality of medical record documentation;
- completeness of medical record documentation;
- release of information (ROI); and
- record retention and storage.

Your compliance committee should create a list of criteria or questions to measure each of the firms interviewed to provide your organization's HIM compliance audit. For some suggestions on what to include, see Exhibit 7.1, "Checklist of Criteria for Auditing Firms."

The compliance audit

The remainder of **Step 7** addresses portions of the audits for each HIM function. Just as they should be monitored regularly, these HIM functions should be formally audited each year:
- content and quality of documentation;
- completeness of documentation;
- coding and abstracting;
- ROI; and
- record retention and storage.

Exhibit 7.1

Checklist of Criteria for Auditing Firms

Name of firm: _____

1. Does your firm have past experience auditing any of the following?
   - ❏ All billing functions
   - ❏ All coding functions
   - ❏ Medical record documentation content and quality
   - ❏ Medical record documentation completeness
   - ❏ Release of information (ROI)
   - ❏ Record retention and storage
   - ❏ Other _____
   - ❏ Other _____

2. What are the credentials of staff performing these functions?
   - ❏ Registered record administrator (RRA)
   - ❏ Accredited record technician (ART)
   - ❏ Certified coding specialist (CCS)
   - ❏ Certified coding specialist—physician-based (CCS-P)
   - ❏ Certified professional coder (CPC)
   - ❏ Certified professional coder-hospital (CPC-H).
   - ❏ Other _____
   - ❏ Other _____

3. Are the individuals performing the functions employees of the firm?
   ❏ Yes ❏ No

4. Has the firm ever charged a contingency fee to audit any of the above functions? (If, yes, they should be eliminated.)
   ❏ Yes ❏ No

5. Does the firm use computerized tools to select samples, store data, and generate reports?
   ❏ Yes: _____
   ❏ No

Exhibit 7.1 *continued*

Checklist of Criteria for Auditing Firms

6. What specific compliance resources does the firm have?
   - ❑ Former compliance officers on staff
   - ❑ Attorneys with criminal defense experience on staff
   - ❑ Attorneys with a healthcare background on staff
   - ❑ Other _____
   - ❑ Other _____

7. What kind of follow-up services can the firm provide if deficiencies are identified?
   - ❑ Coder education
   - ❑ Physician education
   - ❑ Nurse education
   - ❑ Ancillary provider education
   - ❑ Coder documentation
   - ❑ Physician documentation
   - ❑ Nurse documentation
   - ❑ Ancillary provider documentation
   - ❑ Writing and coding policies and procedures
   - ❑ Other _____
   - ❑ Other _____

8. How do you address the issue of providing audit services to a healthcare provider when you also provide some other type of ongoing work (e.g., ROI) for them? Do you have a separate auditing group?

   _____
   _____
   _____
   _____
   _____
   _____

We will address these issues:
- sample selection;
- record review/data element collection;
- reporting and preserving information;
- changing policies and procedures; and
- educating on results.

Sample selection

A portion of your compliance audit sample should be focused—driven by results of your ongoing monitoring activities as well as current government initiatives. And, a percentage of your audit should be a statistically significant random sample to ensure that it addresses high-risk areas as well as other potential internal patterns of at-risk activity. Depending on the area you are auditing, you need to ensure that the focused portion of your reviews reflects a statistically significant sampling of

- service types;
- clinician types;
- patient encounter types;
- high, medium, and low charges (proportionate to risk);
- diagnoses and procedures;
- diagnosis-related group (DRG)/major diagnostic category (MDC) assignment for inpatient cases; and
- ambulatory surgery center (ASC)/ambulatory patient group (APG) assignment for outpatient cases.

You also need to clearly document the methodology used for choosing the sample selection, as well as your rationale for the selection. This information should become part of the permanent audit report.

Special considerations

You need to include a retrospective review piece in your audit for content and quality of documentation and for completeness of documentation. This review should include both a focused and a random sampling of patient records driven by charges. This portion of the audit is a comparison of patient documentation with actual charges. This closes the loop of the documentation review process. During the concurrent monitoring process, you cannot track this piece of data because the charges have not yet been generated.

ROI and record retention audit sample selection can be primarily random. However, for ROI, you should include every record type with specific or additional ROI requirements. For record retention, you should include every type of patient encounter.

Record review/data element collection
The auditing process is a formal review that should identify multiple trends, causes, and possible solutions. As such, you need to collect various data elements to help you to provide this detailed level of information. Generate the data elements as part of a computerized database to ensure that multiple cases and comparisons with different time periods are tracked. These are some data elements that you might want to track during the process:
- the type of document change or error;
- the reason for the change or error;
- the cost of the error to the organization;
- the type of clinician making the error;
- the origin of the error (name of service or physician); and
- the guideline or law cited as an authority for the basis of the change.

Reporting and preserving information
You should preserve audit information in such a manner that you can recreate the entire audit process based upon the preserved

documentation. The reporting process should include, at a minimum, the elements contained in Figure 7.2.

Changing policies and procedures

Your audit firm should include a review of the policies and procedures that relate to the audited area or function. The final report should also include your recommendations for modifying procedures, which might need to be changed for these reasons:
- to ensure that the policies and procedures are an accurate depiction of the activity;
- to reduce compliance risk going forward; and
- to provide staff with accurate documentation to help them to perform consistently.

Policies and procedures can often serve as your compliance plan, especially at the department level. Written policies and procedures guide all activities performed in your department. They take the standards of conduct a step closer to the everyday functioning of HIM staff members. Therefore, it is important to ensure that they are accurate, consistent, and regularly updated. They should be readily available to all involved staff members. Through your actions, you can ensure that policies and procedures guide your department's activities.

Educating on results

Post-audit education is one of the most valuable compliance activities. This is the culmination of one cycle of compliance activity followed by the beginning of the next cycle. Post-audit education should be conducted by the audit firm—an outside, objective party drawing upon actual experience in the organization (through the audit). You need to have high expectations for the post-audit education that your external firm conducts; the educational activity should carry with it the highest credibility and the most focused curriculum.

Exhibit 7.2

> **Data Elements to Record and Preserve**
>
> Record and preserve these data elements during the reporting process:
> - an executive summary of results;
> - the details of the purpose for the review;
> - a sample selection methodology;
> - a record review;
> - a numerical analysis of findings;
> - aggregate reports of data element collection;
> - a narrative analysis of findings;
> - any recommendations; and
> - any plans for follow-up.

Determine your organization's specific compliance educational objectives before contracting with an external firm. At a minimum, the firm should be able to

- provide feedback of audit results to all involved employees;
- conduct interactive training sessions designed to curtail any non-compliant behavior identified in the audit;
- involve physicians, ancillary providers, and other clinical staff in documentation and related areas in a way that makes effective use of their time and addresses key issues;
- provide educational "tools" to coding staff, other HIM staff, clinicians, and billing staff;
- provide all involved employees with action items for improvement; and
- tie in all education to the organization's specific standards of conduct.

Compliance auditing review

You have learned the following in this step:

- Conduct auditing only if your organization is fully embracing compliance—you need to be ready to act on any noncompliant activity identified through an audit.

- The attorney-client privilege used to "protect" audits is a very fragile privilege.

- Conduct comprehensive due diligence on any external firm that you engage to perform compliance auditing.

- Conduct sample selection by giving much thought and consideration to the specific needs and characteristics of your organization.

- Preserve all audit information carefully and accurately.

- Tailor education to the findings of your audit.

- Perform follow-up audits to determine if identified problems have improved.

Epilogue

— **Epilogue** —

Once you complete your first compliance auditing process, you will come full circle in the compliance process. In **Step 1: Understanding the Big Picture,** we discussed the "four pillars" of compliance—education, monitoring, auditing, and the plan/policies and procedures. These pillars need to operate around the core "standards of conduct" discussed in **Step 3.**

More importantly, however, each of these functions interacts synergistically with the others. We saw how standards of conduct are the basis for more detailed policies and procedures. And, that monitoring and auditing will assist you in identifying areas that you need to focus on for education—namely, the five risk areas of
- content and quality of documentation;
- completeness of documentation;
- coding and abstracting;
- release of information; and
- record retention and storage.

You should conduct the functions of education, monitoring, auditing, and updating of policies and procedures on an ongoing, cyclical basis in your department. These activities—combined with the ongoing application of changes in the laws, guidelines, and regulations that govern your organization—make up the formula that will help you to maintain HIM compliance.

Related Products from Opus Communications, The Greeley Company, and The Greeley Education Company

Books
- Compliance Across the Continuum—A Comprehensive Look at Health Care Corporate Compliance
- Continuous Quality Improvement for Health Information Management
- Corporate Compliance: Self-Assessment and Planning
- Information Management: The Compliance Guide to the JCAHO Standards, Second Edition
- Mastering Records Completion: Successful Strategies from Medical Records Briefing
- Netpractice™: A Beginner's Guide to Healthcare Networking on the Internet
- 12 Weeks to a Successful Data Dictionary

Newsletters
- Briefings on Coding Compliance Strategies
- Corporate Compliance Officer
- Health Information Management Across the Continuum
- Medical Records Briefing
- Physician Practice Compliance Report

Videos
- It's Everybody's Job—A Team-Based Approach to Medical Records Completion
- Keep it to Yourself! Protecting Patient Confidentiality
- Understanding Corporate Compliance

Seminars
- Corporate Compliance for Medical Staff Leaders
- Call The Greeley Education Company at 800/801-6661 for complete seminar registration information.

Consulting Services
- Call The Greeley Company at 781/639-8030 for more information on corporate compliance consulting services.

To offer any comments or suggestions, to obtain additional information, or to order any of the above products, please contact us at:

Opus Communications
PO Box 1168
Marblehead, MA 01945

Toll-free telephone: 800/650-6787
Toll-free fax: 800/639-8511
E-mail: customer_service@opuscomm.com
Internet: www.opuscomm.com